Hemant R. Dani obtained
Bombay in April 1949 and
study professional accountan
I.C.W.A., Final Part B in April 1957.

From 1952 to 1977 Mr. Dani worked in various
capacities in Bombay State Road Transport; Grindlay
Abrasives Ltd., Bombay, and *Financial Express*,
Bombay. He then joined Blitz Publications where he
was Assistant Editor from 1981-1986. Subsequently he
was Editor, *Shree Profits* (1986-88) and Chief Executive
and Editor, *Fortune India* (1988-1991).

Mr. Dani also regularly wrote articles on finance and
investments in *Business India, Investor's World, Dalal
Street* and *Island*.

his Miss [Mabel] from

with 19.. and then went to England to

embassy ... where he cleared his.

BALANCE SHEETS
Contents, Analysis & Interpretation

Hemant R. Dani

VISION BOOKS
(Incorporating Orient Paperbacks)
New Delhi • Mumbai • Hyderabad

ISBN 81-7094-373-6

Published in 2000
by
Vision Books Pvt. Ltd.
(Incorporating Orient Paperbacks and CARING Imprints)
24 Feroze Gandhi Road, Lajpat Nagar-III,
New Delhi-110024, India
Phone: (+91-11) 6836470/80
Fax: (+91-11) 6836490
e-mail: visionbk@ vsnl.com

Printed at
Rashtra Rachna Printers
C-88 Ganesh Nagar, Pandav Nagar Complex
Delhi-110092, India

Contents

Preface

This book is the outcome of the author's nearly four decades of experience in the analysis and interpretation of corporate financial statements and was first published by him privately in 1974 with the title *Balance Sheets and How to Read Them*. The book was addressed primarily to laypersons rather than to professional accountants and was so well received that the edition could be completely sold out mainly through mail-order within a relatively short time.

A second edition was planned and the manuscript was thoroughly revised to incorporate the many suggestions received from accountants, financial analysts, and bankers. The proposed edition could not be brought out, however, owing to the author's preoccupation and other reasons. For the present edition, the draft has been revised afresh in the light of the changes statutorily introduced in corporate financial reporting during the last twenty-five years.

As with the first edition, the book is divided into two parts under the same cover. Part One comprising the first fourteen chapters, describes the form and contents of the balance sheet and the profit and loss account — the basic financial statements of commercial and industrial business undertakings. The book being addressed to the layman, the reader is not expected to possess previous knowledge of accountancy. All of the basic concepts and the score or so technical terms used by trained accountants have been explained in simple and non-technical language.

In Part Two (Chapters 15 through 26) the reader is introduced to the technique of "reading" the financial statements with understanding, that is, how to analyse the financial data presented and to draw logical and reliable conclusions from the analysis. All of the methods of analysis commonly employed have been discussed with reference to published annual reports (not necessarily the most recent) of large and reputed public limited companies which have been mentioned under presumed names.

The contents of Part Two are more advanced, but the language used remains largely non-technical and the layman can still follow the discussion with the help of what has been explained in Part One. Part Two is truly meant for the practising accountant, financial analyst and banker and could be, hopefully, of help to students preparing themselves for the various university and professional examinations.

HEMANT R. DANI

PART I

Form and Contents

CHAPTER 1

What Is a Balance Sheet

A balance sheet is the first of the two principal financial statements — the other one being the profit and loss account — forming part of the annual report of an industrial and commercial business undertaking. It is simply a schedule listing values of the assets owned and amounts of the liabilities contracted by an individual, a partnership, an association of persons, or a company registered under the Companies Act, as these appear in the books of account of the business as at a particular date, now by law March 31 of every year.

Assets are the physical property, movable or immovable, cash or its equivalent, and amounts receivable from clients, customers and others having business relationship with the concern. Liabilities are the debts, obligations, and amounts payable to trade creditors, and others. If each of the financial transactions effected during an accounting period is correctly recorded, the total of assets or resources of the business, always equals or "balances" with the total of liabilities or claims.

But, it is not from this accounting inevitability that, the balance sheet derives its title. A balance sheet is so called because it lists, both on the assets side and the liabilities side, the "closing balances" struck in the ledgers at the end of the accounting period which is normally of twelve months' duration, when posting of financial transactions has been completed.

When viewed merely as a financial schedule listing the rupee amounts of assets and liabilities, the balance sheet has little significance and nothing worthwhile can be gained by studying the constituent items unless the business entity to which it relates is being wound up either on the order of a High Court of Judicature or on its going into voluntary liquidation. In this situation, a balance sheet at best provides an estimate of the funds which can be realised on the disposal of assets to meet the claims of creditors.

But, it is a totally different matter if the balance sheet is looked at as a financial snapshot of a real, living and ever-changing business enterprise. The balance sheet of such a "going" concern does no longer appear as a mere list of cold, apparently unrelated, figures. It becomes a living document having a story to tell, a message to deliver to the owners, shareholders, managers, employees, bankers, trade creditors, clients, customers and investors.

Exhibit 1

MULTIPRODUCTS LIMITED
Balance Sheet as at March 31, 20___

LIABILITIES	20___ (Rs)	20___ (Rs)	ASSETS	20___ (Rs)	20___ (Rs)
SHARE CAPITAL:			FIXED ASSETS (See schedule attached)		
AUTHORISED:			Gross		
Preference			*Less:* Depreciation		
Ordinary					
			Capital Work-in Progress		
ISSUED & SUBSCRIBED:			INVESTMENTS:		
Preference			TRADE:		
Ordinary			Quoted		
			Unquoted		
RESERVES & SURPLUS:			CURRENT ASSETS &		
CAPITAL RESERVES:			LOANS AND ADVANCES:		
Share Premium Account			(A) CURRENT ASSETS		
Other Reserves			Stores and Spare Parts		
REVENUE RESERVES:			Loose Tools		
General Reserve			Stock-in-Trade —		
Investment Allowance Reserve			Raw Materials		
Dividend Equalisation Reserve			Work-in-progress		
Retiring Gratuity Reserve			Finished Goods		

Contd...

Exhibit 1 (Contd...)

MULTIPRODUCTS LIMITED
Balance Sheet as at March 31, 20__

LIABILITIES	20__ (Rs)	20__ (Rs)
SECURED LOANS:		
Industrial Finance Corporation		
Loans and Advances from Bank		
UNSECURED LOANS:		
Fixed Deposits		
Other Loans		
CURRENT LIABILITIES & PROVISIONS:		
(A) CURRENT LIABILITIES:		
Acceptances		
Sundry Creditors		
Unclaimed Dividends		
Interest Accrued		
(B) PROVISIONS:		
Taxation		

ASSETS	20__ (Rs)	20__ (Rs)
Sundry Debtors —		
Good		
Doubtful		
Cash —		
On Hand		
With Bank		
(B) LOANS AND ADVANCES		
Advances Recoverable in		
Cash or in Kind —		
Secured		
Unsecured		

To be able to read the story, or to decipher the message, one has to be conversant with the language it has been delivered in. Like all professional people, accountants have developed over the centuries a specialised vocabulary which, most of the time, is easy to understand but, at times, plain confusing. Luckily, there are only a score or so technical terms which have to be got straight in the mind and once they are, the business of reading a balance sheet ceases to appear as formidable and painful an undertaking as it does at first sight.

This does not mean, however, that whoever wants to read a balance sheet with understanding has to undergo a course in double entry book-keeping and must know how to construct a balance sheet from the list of closing balances. After all, to appreciate a piece of art one does not have to be an artist oneself. To be able to read it intelligently and accurately, one need only to be familiar with the general layout of a balance sheet, understand fully what every element from which it has been built up stands for, and develop the ability to perceive the relationship which the balance sheet figures bear to each other in the context of the total business activity.

Balance Sheet — General Layout

Balance sheets, so far as the details carried by them are concerned, are as varied as the business activities they represent. But, from the point of view of their general layout, they can either be horizontal or vertical as made mandatory by the Companies Act. The horizontal or columnar form is the traditional one and is simpler for the layperson to understand because it diagrammatically represents the definition of a balance sheet as being a financial schedule of assets and liabilities.

A typical balance sheet in the horizontal form is presented as Exhibit 1 wherein figures have been omitted for the sake of convenience.

When the items to be included are numerous, companies have the liberty to present the balance in a summarised form and then provide the relevant details in schedules or annexures. Thus, schedules may be included to show details of the authorised, issued and paid-up share capitals; reserves and surplus; secured and unsecured loans; current liabilities and provisions; fixed assets less accumulated depreciation; trade and other investments with their cost of purchase and market values on the date of the balance sheet, and current assets, loans and advances. A typical summarised balance sheet is shown in Exhibit 2.

The other style of presenting a balance sheet which, too, has the sanction of Schedule VI of the Companies Act, is vertical instead of being horizontal. This appears as Exhibit 3. It will be observed that the

Exhibit 2

MULTIPRODUCTS LIMITED
Balance Sheet as at March 31, 20___

LIABILITIES	Annexure	This Year Rs	Previous Year Rs	ASSETS	Annexure	This Year Rs	Previous Year Rs
SHARE CAPITAL	1			FIXED ASSETS	5		
RESERVES & SURPLUS	2			INVESTMENTS	6		
LOANS	3			CURRENT ASSETS, LOANS AND ADVANCES	7		
CURRENT LIABILITIES & PROVISIONS	4						
CONTINGENT LIABILITIES & NOTES	8						

Exhibit 3

MULTI PRODUCTS LTD

Balance Sheet as at March 31, 20__

	Schedule No.	Current Year	previous year
1. SOURCES OF FUNDS			
(1) Shareholders' Funds:			
(a) Capital			
(b) Reserves and Surplus			
(2) Loan Funds:			
(a) Secured Loans			
(b) Unsecured Loans		_____	_____
Total		_____	_____
2. APPLICATION OF FUNDS			
(1) Fixed Assets:			
(a) Gross Block			
(b) Less: Depreciation			
(c) Net Block			
(d) Capital work-in-progress			
(2) Investments			
(3) Current Assets, Loans and Advances :			
(a) Inventories			
(b) Sundry Debtors			
(c) Cash and Bank Balances			
(d) Other Current Assets			
(e) Loans and Advances			
Less : Current Liabilities & Provisions :			
(a) Liabilities			
(b) Provisions			
Net Current Assets			
(4) (a) Miscellaneous Expenditure not written off			
(b) Profit and Loss Account		_____	_____
Total			

financial data supplied are just the same as in the traditional horizontal or columnar form of Exhibit 1 except that they have been arranged to show:

1. The total amount of capital or funds invested in the business and how much of it has been provided by the owners themselves. The amount invested by the members is called "Shareholders' Funds" or, more commonly, the "Net Worth" of the company and equals the total of the share capital and the reserves. The statement or

columnar form of presenting the balance sheet thus reveals the extent of the interest of the owners themselves in the business.
2. The distribution of total funds among the different types of assets, such as fixed assets, miscellaneous assets, and current assets. Fixed assets are assets like land, buildings, plant, machinery and equipment which are held more or less permanently. Current assets include stocks of raw materials, work-in-progress and finished goods, trade debtors, marketable securities and cash. Such assets are held only temporarily and, with the exception of short-term investments, are convertible into cash by successive steps in the normal operations of the business.

Exhibit 4

MULTI PRODUCTS LIMITED
Balance Sheet as at March 31, 20__

		20__	20__
NET ASSETS EMPLOYED			
Fixed Assets			
At Cost *less* Depreciation	(1)		
Capital work-in-progress	_____		
Investments	(2)		
Net Current Assets			
Current Assets			
Loans & Advances	(3)		
Stocks, Stores & Spare Parts	(4)		
Debtors	(5)		
Cash & Bank Balances	(6) _____		
Less			
Current Liabilities & Provisions			
Creditors, Other Liabilities			
and Provisions	(7)		
Taxation	_____		
		========	=======
SOURCES OF FINANCE			
Share Capital and Reserves			
Share Capital	(8)		
Reserves & Surplus	(9) _____		
Loan Capital	(10)		
Bank & Other Loans	(11) _____		
		_____	_____
		========	=======

(Figures in brackets refer to Notes which form part of the Balance Sheet).

A variation of the above form is presented in Exhibit 4. Here the order is reversed. Net assets employed in the business are shown first and the total funds invested in them thereafter. Net assets are all assets less current liabilities, that is, assets purchased or acquired out of funds provided by the owners and suppliers of long-term credit.

Net assets include fixed assets less depreciation, capital work-in-progress, long-term investments, and net current assets, that is, current assets less current liabilities. The major sources of funds are : share capital, reserves, loan stock such as debentures and similar securities, and bank and other loans or borrowings.

CHAPTER 2

What Does a Balance Sheet Tell Us

The financial position of a company as a going concern is never stationary and is in the process of continuous change. Raw materials are purchased and converted into finished goods which, in turn, are sold. Money constantly flows in as sales are effected and customers pay their dues. On the other hand, cash gets regularly depleted as wages and other expenses incidental to the business are paid, purchases of raw materials and essential supplies are made, and suppliers' bills are settled on due dates. The book value of many of the assets and liabilities as shown on the balance sheet, thus, undergoes a constant change.

To portray these changes as they take place, it becomes necessary to maintain a continuous record of the financial transactions as they take place. To ascertain the financial position of a company as at a particular point of time, the process of recording has to be temporarily halted. A balance sheet, then, is the picture which emerges when the process of recording financial transactions is so arrested.

This does not mean that, to get a static snapshot of its financial position as on a particular day, the company has to temporarily halt all its operations as is done by some large retailers when they down their shutters for a couple of days for the purpose of the annual stock-taking. All that the company need do is to maintain separate books of account for individual years and stop making further entries in the books pertaining to the year that has just ended unless the transactions specifically relate to that year. Once all the entries are completed, the books can be closed and balances struck which then can be transferred to the balance sheet to show the financial standing of the company as on the last day of the year.

A balance sheet can be prepared after the passage of any predetermined length of time. For example, balance sheets can be drawn up at the end of each month, quarter, six-months or a year. The law leaves companies free to decide how frequently they would like to prepare their balance sheets and only requires that the so-called 'financial year', which may be less or more than a calendar year, shall not exceed fifteen months.

Since, however, it is both expensive and inconvenient to prepare balance sheets at frequent short intervals, companies invariably prefer to prepare balance sheets at the end of each period of twelve months.

The yearly balance sheet is, thus, the one most commonly met with and has the advantage that it covers all of the seasons of the years.

Now, the financial year of a company may commence on any date and end on the preceding date a year later. Here again, the law had once preferred not to interfere except in some cases where the companies concerned were required to prepare balance sheets to show their financial status as on a prescribed date each year.

Commercial banks, for instance, were required to prepare their balance sheets as at December 31; electrical undertakings, public utilities and general insurance companies as at March 31; and co-operative societies as at June 30. The rest of the companies were left free to choose their financial years as they liked. The situation has changed and all companies are required by law to draw up their balance sheets as at March 31 of each year. In other words, they all have to adopt the financial year (April 1 to March 31) as their accounting year.

Some companies had once adopted a trading year of 52 weeks divided into 13 periods of four weeks each. This scheme was introduced to avoid the noncompatibility of monthly financial reports using the irregular calendar months which vary in length from 28 to 31 days. A notable example of this was Guest, Keen Williams Ltd.

Plantation companies or those using agricultural produce as raw material — sugar companies, for instance — had adopted the natural year as their trading year. Sugar factories in Maharashtra and South India start crushing operations after the end of the monsoon when the sugarcane crop is ready for harvesting. Their trading year, therefore, used to begin on October 1 and end on September 30 the next year.

The natural business year of such companies, thus, coincided with the cycle of operations. The annual operating cycle terminated, when the business activity was at the lowest ebb and when inventories, receivables, and liabilities were reduced to their minimum. To put it differently, the trading year ended at a time when activity had been reduced to a low point and the business was at its "most liquid state".

As mentioned in Chapter 1, a balance sheet in its traditional form is a columnar statement of the financial position or status of a company. The statement is prepared by listing liabilities on the left-hand side and assets on the right-hand side. Balance sheets so prepared break down naturally into four firm divisions — two on the liabilities side and two on the assets side as shown in Exhibit 5.

The first division on the liabilities side comprises all "permanent" liabilities in the nature of the share capital and accumulated reserves. The second division covers all temporary liabilities and can be further split into two sub-divisions. The first sub-division includes all long-term or "non-current" liabilities such as debenture bonds, long-term

Exhibit 5

Major Divisions of a Balance Sheet

LIABILITIES	ASSETS
SHARE CAPITAL & RESERVES (NET WORTH)	FIXED ASSETS
	INTANGIBLES
	LONG-TERM INVESTMENTS
LONG-TERM LOANS	MISCELLANEOUS ASSETS
MISCELLANEOUS LIABILITIES	CURRENT ASSETS
CURRENT LIABILITIES	

loans from banks or financial institutions, and miscellaneous deferred liabilities.

The second sub-division is made up of current liabilities, that is, obligations which must be met, by convention, within one year from the date of the balance sheet. Such obligations or accounts consist of trade creditors, bank overdrafts or cash credits, deposits from clients against goods to be supplied or from the public as short-term loans, accrued interest, salaries and wages, rates and taxes, unclaimed dividends and the such.

The two divisions on the assets-side consist of "current" and "non-current" assets. The distinction between current and non-current assets is relative and depends on the ease and frequency with which an asset can be converted into cash. Some assets like land, buildings, plant and machinery are employed continuously and remain in their particular form or shape until depreciated, sold off, thrown away or pulled down.

Similarly, investments in other companies, quoted or unquoted, which are held as a matter of trade policy, remain on the books of the company at their purchase price until written down or disposed of.

Such assets are "fixed" or almost permanent in nature and, so, are included among non-current assets.

There are certain types of assets which, in the legal sense, have no material existence and are called "intangibles". Their real value is dependent upon the contribution they make to the earnings in the business. Included among such assets are goodwill, patents, copyrights, brand names, secret processes, formulas, leases, and so on. They appear on the balance sheets of only large companies and are frequently written down to a nominal amount.

There are other assets which are essentially cash, invested cash, or physical assets which are going to be converted into cash within a comparatively shorter time in the normal course of business. These are current assets and include stocks of raw materials, work-in-progress as at the end of the year, stock of finished goods, trade debtors, temporary marketable investments and cash.

Alternatively, a balance sheet may be viewed as a statement of investment listing, first, the various sources of funds and, then, the different types of assets in which these funds have been invested. The balance sheet in Exhibit 3 has been prepared from this angle. It, first, sets out the net amount of capital funds obtained from each of the several sources and, then, goes on to show how these have been employed in acquiring various types of assets.

The sources of capital are listed in the order of their permanency, starting with the capital contributed by the shareholders and followed by reserves, which are retained or ploughed-back profits, and then borrowings. The loans are classified and listed according to their periods of maturity, the long-term loans taking precedence over the shorter-term ones.

The assets, likewise, are listed according to their permanency and in the reverse order of the ease with which they can be converted into cash. Fixed assets such as land, buildings, plant and machinery which are held more or less permanently, are listed first and are followed by the slow moving assets and finally by the quick or current assets.

In this form of presenting a balance sheet, current assets are always shown "net", that is, after deducting therefrom the total of current liabilities. The reason is that at least some of the current assets are purchased with funds made available by short-term creditors like banks who advance loans, and suppliers who extend credit. To get at the correct amount of the long-term finance invested in short-term or current assets it is necessary to deduct from the amount of current assets the amount of current or short-term liabilities.

Details which cannot be conveniently accommodated in the balance sheet but are considered pertinent or essential are shown in footnotes or separate schedules which are made an integral part of the balance sheet. The law also requires companies to provide some additional information for the benefit of shareholders, creditors and others doing business with the companies. Topics usually mentioned in appended notes or annexures include:

➤ Details regarding redemption of preference shares and debenture bonds, and repayment of long-term or special loans,
➤ Dividends declared payable out of reserves,
➤ Provisions for taxation or contingencies,
➤ Changes in accounting practices, depreciation policies, and valuation methods,
➤ Estimated amount of contracts remaining to be completed on capital account,
➤ Arrears of preference dividends and depreciation,
➤ Description and amounts of contingent liabilities,
➤ Explanation regarding payment of retiring gratuity, or pension,
➤ Comment on extraordinary gains or losses,
➤ Computation of managerial remuneration and commission,
➤ Quantitative details of licences and installed capacities for manufacture of main products, actual production and main raw materials consumed,
➤ Details of events materially affecting the financial position as revealed by the balance sheet, that occurred or became known after the close of the year in question.

CHAPTER 3

Who Is Interested in Balance Sheets and Why

Having seen what balance sheets are, the various forms in which they can be presented, and the message they carry, it may be inquired, "Who is interested in balance sheets and why?" The answer is that there are many groups of people in different walks of life who have reasons to be interested in, or to be concerned with, balance sheets of business enterprises. The major groups are:

(i)   Governmental Regulatory Bodies,
(ii) Trade Associations,
(iii) Stock Exchanges,
(iv) Shareholders and Investors,
(v)   Banks, Financial Institutions and General Creditors,
(vi) Employees, and
(vii) Management.

Governmental Regulatory Bodies

Every private and public limited company is required by law to file three copies of its balance sheet and profit and loss account with the Registrar of Companies within thirty days from the date of the annual general meeting in which the balance sheet and the profit and loss account have been approved and adopted by the shareholders.

The purpose behind this requirement is to ensure that the balance sheet and the profit and loss account have been prepared as near as possible to the form prescribed by the Companies Act and give a true and fair picture of the state of affairs of the company. In other words the main purpose is to safeguard the interest of the shareholders and to see that they are supplied with adequate information regarding the operations and state of finance of their company.

The Income Tax Department

Is another Governmental agency to which a copy of the published balance sheet and profit and loss account must be supplied by each company while submitting its income-tax return.

Trade Associations

A trade association is a non-profit organisation of companies or firms in the same trade or line of business formed for the purpose of protecting the interest of its members. The association sometimes obtains balance sheets of its member companies and firms and, through the mechanism of inter-firm ratios, tries to compare the competitive position of different firms. At times, the associations may design uniform systems of accounting for use by their members for the sake of better inter-firm comparison.

Stock Exchanges

Companies seeking price quotations and trading facilities for their stocks and shares, are required to enter into "listing agreements" with the concerned stock exchanges. Under these agreements, the companies are required to file with the stock exchanges six copies of statutory reports, directors' annual reports, balance sheets, profit and loss accounts and all periodical and special reports, as soon as they are ready; six copies of all notices, resolutions and circulars relating to new issues of capital prior to their despatch to shareholders; three copies of all notices, call-letters or any other circulars at the same time as they are sent to shareholders or debentureholders are advertised in the press. The principal objective is to secure a full and fair disclosure of the financial position and the value of the listed securities in the interest of the trading public.

Shareholders and Investors

Shareholders who are the members and owners of a company or firm are interested in knowing how the capital provided by them has been invested in the assets of the company, the debts and the obligations of the firm, the profits earned during a year and their disposal. They analyse the balance sheet and the profit and loss account to evaluate the profitability or otherwise of operations of the business.

Investors who intend to purchase preference or ordinary shares or debenture bonds of a company are concerned principally with the prospective earning power and the working capital position which is considered indicative of solvency. Prospective buyers of debenture bonds are also interested in the property or fixed assets which are secured against the debenture loan.

Shareholders and prospective investors are primarily concerned with the future earning power of companies because such earnings are the funds from which fixed charges like interest on borrowings and dividend on preference shares can be paid, loans can be repaid, future renovations and expansions can be financed without fresh borrowings or refinancing, and dividends can be distributed on ordinary shares.

The assessment of earning power calls for consideration of a number of factors which are not necessarily revealed in the balance sheet or the profit and loss account such as the conditions prevailing in and future prospects for various industries and the calibre of management. The method of analysing the balance sheet and the profit and loss account with a view to estimating future earning power of a company is known as "Investment Analysis".

Banks, Financial Institutions and General Creditors

General creditors like banks and suppliers of goods and services, provide short-term credit to a business and are primarily concerned with liquidity and the borrower's ability to meet his short-term obligations. They tend to place greater emphasis on a study of the balance sheet rather than of the profit and loss account, and carefully weigh the ratio of current assets to current liabilities and the adequacy of working capital. Their approach goes by the name of "Credit Analysis".

Employees

Next only to the management, the employees of a company have reason to be intimately concerned with its prosperity. They look forward to receiving higher wages and salaries, welfare benefits, better working conditions, shorter working hours, health, insurance and retirement benefits, and, of course, the yearly bonus. They, or their spokesmen, study the financial statements to find out how their company has progressed and what its immediate prospects are. Since it is difficult to find suitable alternative jobs, it is but natural that employees should be intimately concerned with the future of their company.

Management

Present-day business concerns are large-scale organisations the operations of which are controlled by professional managers. These persons operate the business for the owners who are many hundreds of shareholders spread throughout the country. They are directly responsible for improving the efficiency and profitability of the business.

Because of the large scale of operations, it becomes difficult for top management to keep personal relationship with each production or operating department. To maintain and improve the efficiency of the business, therefore, management has to depend largely upon periodic financial, operating, and statistical reports.

The annual report comprising the balance sheet and the profit and loss account is but one, though the most important, of such reports. Supplementary detailed managerial internal operating reports are prepared at short intervals to measure costs of various activities, efficiencies of different departments, divisions or processes, efficiency of individuals in responsible positions and for many other purposes.

CHAPTER 4

Share Capital and How It Is Raised

No matter what is the nature of its business, every industrial and commercial enterprise must have capital to finance its undertaking. It must have money to purchase land, construct factory and other buildings; buy plant, machinery and equipment, and to provide for what is called the working capital, that is, funds required to meet day-to-day expenses of the business. The capital may be "owned", that is, provided entirely by the owners of the undertaking, or a part of it may be "borrowed", that is, obtained in the form of a loan from financial institutions, banks and, not infrequently, the public.

Proprietary firms, partnerships and private limited companies must raise their capital privately because of the restrictions imposed on them by law. In the case of proprietary or self-owned concerns, the whole of the capital is introduced by the proprietor or owner. In the case of partnerships of two or more people, the capital is contributed by the partners in equal or in agreed proportion and the gains and losses of the business are also shared in the same proportion.

A private limited company obtains its capital from its members the total number of whom cannot be less than two and more than fifty excluding employees, past and present. The capital required to be raised is split into a number of parts called "shares" which are sold for cash to the persons who wish to join the company. Each share has the same "par" or "face" value which, in theory, can be anything, but official guidelines now require all companies to fix it at Rs 10. This is, of course, printed on each share certificate.

If more capital is later required, a further number of shares having the same face value is offered for sale, at par or at a premium, to the existing shareholders strictly in proportion to their current holdings so as not to disturb the extent of their ownership of the business.

If need be, shares may be offered to employees and even though this widens the sphere from which capital can be raised, it still remains restricted. A public limited company is more fortunately placed in this respect because it can offer its shares for sale to the vast multitude of people by following the rules laid down in this regard by the Securities and Exchange Board of India (SEBI).

But before a company, whether private limited or public limited, can raise capital through an issue of shares, its "Articles of Association" must "authorise" such an issue. How much share capital the Articles should authorise the company to raise will depend on the promoters' estimate of the funds that would be needed for their business. Any figure may be mentioned keeping in mind future requirements as well as the cost of registration which is related to the amount of the authorised share capital.

But once a figure has been incorporated in the Articles, the company will not be permitted to raise a share capital in excess of this amount which is now its "Authorised" or "Nominal" share capital. If it becomes necessary to increase the share capital beyond this limit, the company must get its Articles amended and the authorised share capital suitably raised.

A Company need not raise the whole of the authorised share capital all at the same time. It may raise a part initially and more as the need arises. It has been mentioned earlier that a company raises its capital by issuing shares to its members or the public at large. That part of the share capital which, then, is sought to be raised by issuing shares becomes the "Issued" share capital of the company and may be equal to or less than the authorised share capital.

Each share, as we have seen, has a certain par or face value. It is not necessary that the company should demand the full value of the shares at the time of their issue, although it is not infrequently that the full price is demanded at the time of application. More commonly, however, only a portion of the amount is demanded to start with and the balance is recovered in equal instalments called "Calls".

So long as the full value of the shares is not called-up, the shares remain "partly paid" but become "fully paid" when the full value is called-up and paid. Normally, the issued capital and the paid-up capital (if the shares are fully paid) should be equal. But, since some of the shareholders fail to pay the calls in time, there is generally some difference between the amounts of the two. If the unpaid calls are not paid even after repeated demands, the company has the right to forfeit the shares on giving due notice and, if necessary, to re-issue them at some future date.

Classes of Shares

Now, if the shares issued by a company all have the same rights regarding sharing the gains and losses of the business and participating in the management of the company, they belong to the same class "Ordinary" or "Equity Shares". But, at times, companies find it convenient to issue another class of shares called "Preference Shares" which differ from equity shares in two respects.

First, the holders thereof can have no say in the management of the company save only in matters affecting their rights or, when the stipulated amount of dividend has remained unpaid for two years or more. And, second, with the view to compensating the loss of voting power, the holders are given a preferential position in respect of receipt of dividend and the repayment of the capital amount on the winding-up of the company.

The rate of dividend which is a fixed one, is expressed as a percentage of the nominal or face value of the shares. It is to be noted, however, that not unlike the dividend on equity shares, dividend on preference shares is paid only if there are profits available. If there are no profits, the dividend is either not paid at all or is deferred to a later year when profits are adequate.

Preference shares can be of various types as follows:

1. *Cumulative Preference Shares* are those the dividend on which, if not paid in one year, accumulates and will be paid in a later year before any distribution of profits is made to the equity holders.
2. *Non-cumulative Preference Shares,* which are rather uncommon, do not carry the above right and if no dividend is paid in a year because of absence or inadequacy of profits, it is lost for ever.
3. *Redeemable Preference Shares* are those which carry the right of repayment of the invested capital at a stated price at some future date or dates.
4. *Non-redeemable Preference Shares* do not carry the right of repayment and the capital invested therein is repaid only on the dissolution or winding-up of the company. This class of preference share can no longer be issued, however, because the Companies Act, 1956, lays down that no company can issue any preference share which is totally irredeemable or redeemable after the expiry of a period of eighteen years.
5. *Participating Preference Shares* entitle the holders to dividends in excess of the stipulated amount under specified conditions so as to enable their holders to participate in the growth of the company to some extent at least.
6. *Convertible Preference Shares* provide the holders an option of converting the preference shares into equity shares in a certain proportion and during a specified period.

A company may issue more than one class of any of the above types of preference shares and more than one "series" in each class. It may, for instance, issue, First, Second and Third Redeemable Preference Shares and may have A, B and C series in each of these classes. The rate of dividend payable on all these shares can be the same or can vary from class to class. But the fact to note is that, in the matter of payment of dividend and repayment of capital, First Preference Shares will rank ahead of Second Preference Shares which, in turn, rank ahead of Third Preference Shares and so on.

The same situation once prevailed in the case of equity shares or ordinary shares as they were then labelled. Companies, then, would issue *Preferred Ordinary Shares* which carried dividend and capital repayment rights ahead of the ordinary shares or they could issue *Deferred Ordinary Shares* which carried such rights after the ordinary shares. They could also issue *Deferred or Founders' Shares* which enjoyed certain special rights and privileges and could claim the entire surplus available after dividends were paid on the preference and ordinary shares of all types.

This situation no larger obtains and the Companies Act lays down that "no company formed after the commencement of the Act shall issue any shares (not being preference shares) which carry voting rights or rights in the company as to dividend, capital or otherwise which are disproportionate to the rights attaching to the holders of other shares (not being preference shares)". In other words, redeemable preference shares with their varying types and equity shares are the only classes of shares that companies can issue.

Exhibit 6 shows that portion of a balance sheet concerned with the authorised, issued and paid-up share capital of a company. Figures have been omitted for the sake of convenience.

Exhibit 6

MULTI PRODUCTS LIMITED
Balance Sheet as at March 31, 20___

Previous Year	LIABILITIES	As at March 31, 20___	
	SHARE CAPITAL		
	Authorised :		
	Preference		
	Ordinary		
========		========	========
	Issued :		
	Preference		
	Ordinary		
========		========	========
	Paid-up :		
	Preference		
	Ordinary		
_____	*Less:* Calls unpaid	_____	
_____	*Add:* Shares Forfeited	_____	
	Total Share Capital		
========		========	

CHAPTER 5

The Meaning of Reserves

The second item under the heading "Liabilities" on a balance sheet is "Reserves". In the language of accountancy, this means the excess of assets over liabilities, including the share capital, and is shown immediately after the share capital because such excess or surplus, no matter how derived, belongs to the owners of the company and forms a part of their "equity".

In plain language, reserves are nothing but profits retained, or "ploughed back", in the business and accumulated over the years. They generally fall into two categories depending upon the source from which the retained profits have arisen.

If the retained profits have been derived from the normal trading operations of the business, the reserves created out of them are called "Revenue Reserves". If, on the other hand, the retained profits are of a non-revenue nature and have been derived from non-trading operations of the company, the reserves created out of them are termed "Capital Reserves" and are not to be regarded as free for distribution by way of dividends.

The sources of capital reserves are many and may include:

1. Profits from the sale of fixed assets
2. Profits made prior to incorporation
3. Profits made by a subsidiary prior to its acquisition
4. Profits from the sale of a subsidiary
5. Remission fees on forfeited shares
6. Profits on the redemption of shares and debentures
7. Premium on the issue of debentures
8. Excess arising out of the revaluation of fixed assets.

Gains or profits from all these different sources can be clubbed together and shown under one common heading. There are certain capital reserves, however, which the law requires to be shown separately on the balance sheet. These are:

Share Premium Account. Whenever shares are issued at a premium, that is, at a price above their par or nominal value, the aggregate amount of the premium on these shares is to be credited to a separate account called the "Share Premium Account". For example, if a company issues one lakh equity shares of Rs 10 each at Rs 12 per share, the excess of Rs 2 per share, that is Rs 2,00,000 in aggregate, is transferred to the share premium account. This amount can be used only:

1. In paying up unissued shares of the company to be issued to the members as fully paid bonus shares
2. In writing off the preliminary expenses of the company
3. In writing off the expenses of, or the commission paid, or the discount allowed on any issue of shares or debentures
4. In providing for the premium payable on the redemption of any redeemable preference shares or any debentures
5. If the Share Premium Account is to be dealt in any other way, sanction of a High Court would have to be obtained.

Capital Redemption Reserve. This is a specified reserve created over the years by setting aside a part of the profits earned for the purpose of repaying or redeeming the preference share capital of the company. The only other purpose to which this reserve can by law be put to is to pay up for the unissued shares when such shares are issued as fully paid bonus shares to the members of the company.

Revenue reserves, as already stated, are the trading profits which are retained or ploughed back in the business. They represent the surplus which remains after meeting all expenses of the business, writing off depreciation, providing for corporate taxation and paying dividends on preference and equity shares.

Theoretically, the entire amount of the profit after tax can be distributed as dividend among the shareholders but prudent managements often set aside a part of the available profit to finance future expansion, renovation and replacement of assets, or to meet unexpected expenses.

Revenue reserves like capital reserves can be of two types : "tied" or "specific", and "free" or "general". Specific reserves, as their label describes are created for specific purposes such as repairs of a major nature, renewal or replacement of assets, writing off bad debts, additional depreciation, retirement benefits for employees and so on.

General reserves, on the other hand, are not created for any specific purpose. Some of the types of revenue reserves commonly met with are:

➤ Tax-exempt Profits Reserve,
➤ Contingency Reserve,
➤ Repairs and Renewals Reserve,
➤ Deferred Taxation Reserve,
➤ Dividend Equalisation Reserve,
➤ Bad Debts Reserve,

➤ Additional Depreciation Reserve,
➤ Investment Allowance Reserve,
➤ Retiring Gratuity Reserve,
➤ Investment Reserve, and so on.

The list can be extended to any length and a variety of specific purpose revenue reserves can be created at the will of the directors. The aggregate amount in each of the specific reserves, however, is small compared with the total of reserves and the bulk is to be found in the "General Reserve".

The list of reserves sometimes ends with a "Profit and Loss Balance" which is the small surplus that is carried forward from one accounting period to the next and is, in fact, a part of the general reserve.

The distinction between specific purpose revenue reserves and general purpose revenue reserves is arbitrary and there is nothing in the law to prevent the directors from transferring amounts from one reserve to another. In fact, all revenue reserves are general reserves and can be used freely for payment of dividend and issue of bonus shares. They can be, and frequently are, transferred back to the profit and loss account to strengthen the results of a poor year and to facilitate payment of dividend if that is considered desirable. There is, therefore, no particular merit in segregating revenue reserves in the above manner and the practice is rapidly going out of fashion.

Frequently in this chapter mention was made of companies being free to apply their capital and revenue reserves, with the exception of statutory reserves like the investment allowance reserve, to issue fully-paid bonus shares to their members. In accounting terminology this means "capitalisation" of reserves and the process involves the transfer of a certain amount from the reserves to the share capital. This may be explained with the help of a simple illustration.

Suppose a company has a share capital of Rs 50,00,000 in ordinary shares of Rs 10 each, a share premium account of Rs 5,00,000, an investment allowance reserve of Rs 10,00,000, and a general reserve of Rs 40,00,000. Its balance sheet will show the following position:

	Rs	Rs
SHARE CAPITAL		
Authorised : 10,00,000		
Equity Shares of Rs 10		
Each.		1,00,00,000
Issued and paid-up : 5,00,000		
Equity Shares of Rs 10		
Each		50,00,000

	Rs	Rs
RESERVES & SURPLUS		
Capital Reserve :		
Share Premium Account	5,00,000	
Revenue Reserves :		
Investment Allowance Reserve	10,00,000	
General Reserve	40,00,000	
		55,00,000
Total Share Capital and Reserves		1,05,00,000
		=========

If the company decides to issue bonus shares in the proportion of one bonus share for every five shares already held, it can do so by capitalising the whole of the share premium account, and the general reserve to the extent of Rs 5,00,000. After the issue of bonus shares the balance sheet of the company will show the following position

	Rs	Rs
SHARE CAPITAL		
Authorised : 10,00,000		
Equity Shares of		
Rs 10 each		1,00,00,000
Issued and Paid-up :		
6,00,000 Equity		
Shares of Rs 10 each		60,00,000
(Of the above, 1,00,000		
Equity Shares have been issued		
as fully paid bonus shares)		
RESERVE & SURPLUS		
Revenue Reserves :		
Investment Allowance Reserves	10,00,000	
General Reserve	35,00,000	
		45,00,000
Total Share Capital and Reserves		1,05,00,000
		=========

Note that the total of the share capital and reserves has remained unchanged which is as it should have been because the bonus shares were issued free of cost to the shareholders and no additional cash was brought in as share capital.

In other words, the net worth, or the owners' equity, has undergone no change and it is only the "book-value" or the "break-up value" of each share that has gone down from Rs 21 (Rs 1,05,00,000 divided by the original number of shares, that is, 5,00,000) to Rs 17.50 (Rs 1,05,00,000 divided by the new number of shares, that is, 6,00,000).

The reduction in the book value of a share following an issue of bonus shares really does not mean that a shareholder has suffered a capital loss. This is because the number of shares held by him has gone up proportionately. If before the issue of bonus shares he was holding one hundred shares, his total contribution to the net worth was Rs 2,100 (100 shares worth Rs 21 each). After the issue of bonus shares he would be holding 120 shares each worth in the companies books at Rs 17.50 and his contribution to the net worth would again be Rs 2,100. The experience of every shareholder of the company would be no different.

But the shareholders would suffer an income loss if the rate of dividend per share were to be lowered disproportionately to the ratio in which bonus shares were issued to them. If, for instance, the rate of dividend paid on the original 5,00,000 shares was Rs 1.80 per share, holder of one hundred shares would earn an income of Rs 180 and would earn the same income even if the rate of dividend per share payable on the enlarged (that is 120) number of shares he now owns were to be lowered to Rs 1.50. Any further lowering of the rate would naturally, involve him is a loss of income.

Similarly, the shareholder would suffer a capital loss if the market price of the share were to be marked down disproportionately. If, for instance, the market price of Rs 10 paid share was Rs 45 before the issue of bonus shares, the market valuation of an investor's original holding of one hundred shares would be Rs 4,500. He would not be worse off even if the price were to be lowered to Rs 37.50 on an ex bonus basis. But if the price were to decline more for any reason and the investor were to sell his shares, he would earn a capital loss.

CHAPTER 6

Net Worth or Owners' Equity

The liabilities of a company represent its indebtedness. This indebtedness may be to outsiders such as banks, financial institutions, the public when debentures or bonds are issued or deposits are accepted, and suppliers of goods and services, or, it may be to the owners who provide the necessary capital.

In all properly drawn balance sheets, the accountabilities to outsiders are clearly distinguished from those to the owners or shareholders because in the event of a winding-up, outside creditors must be paid in full before any distribution of cash is made to the owners.

A company's liability to its owners is known variously as "Shareholders' Funds", "Owners Equity" or "Net Worth". The method of stating this liability on the balance sheet depends upon whether the balance sheet is that of a proprietary concern, a partnership or a limited liability company, private or public.

The balance sheet of a firm owned by a single individual will show the owner's equity simply as

Shri K. Capital   Rs 25,000

In the case of a partnership which is an association of two or more individuals, the net worth is shown in several capital accounts, one for each partner. Thus,

Shri A. Capital   Rs 40,000
Shri B. Capital   Rs 35,000
Shri C. Capital   Rs 25,000

It will be observed that there are no reserves because the retained profits attributable to each partner, unless withdrawn, are normally merged with his/her capital.

In the case of a limited liability company, the net worth represents the total of the preference share capital, if any, the equity share capital and reserves and surplus. That part of the balance sheet of a company showing the net worth, that is the total of the different classes of shares and the reserves, is reproduced in Exhibit 7.

The balance sheet presented, dates back to a period when it was not uncommon for companies to raise capital by issuing several classes of preference shares. Since then, preference shares as a class have gone totally out of favour with investors and are rarely issued, if at all. To

---

Exhibit 7

Owners' Equity or Net Worth

			Rs	Rs
SHARE CAPITAL				
	10,000	5 % Cumulative Tax-free Redeemable First Preference Shares of Rs 100 each	10,00,000	
	30,000	6 % Cumulative Tax-free Redeemable Second Preference Shares of Rs 100 each	30,00,000	
	40,000	7 % Cumulative Tax-free Redeemable Third Preference Shares of Rs 100 each	40,00,000	
	29,331	7 % Cumulative Tax-free Redeemable Convertible Third Preference Shares of Rs 100 each	<u>29,33,100</u>	1,09,33,100
14,06,490		Equity Shares of Rs 10 each	1,40,64,900	
1,00,000		'A' Equity Shares of Rs 10 each	<u>10,00,000</u>	<u>1,50,64,900</u>
				2,59,98,000
		Add: Forfeited Amount		550
				2,59,98,550
RESERVES & SURPLUS				
		Capital Reserve	3,85,932	
		Development Rebate Reserve	41,20,000	
		General Reserve	28,69,902	<u>73,75,834</u>
		Total Owners' Equity or Net Worth		3,33,74,384

explain the methodology of computing the net worth of different classes of shares, reference has to be made to balance sheets relating to periods when issuing such shares was a common practice among companies.

It will be noted that the names of owners appear on the balance sheets of proprietary concerns and partnerships but never on those of limited liability companies. There are two reasons for this. First, the number of shareholders or members of limited liability companies is usually so large that their names cannot be, with convenience, mentioned on the balance sheet.

Second, and more important, unlike the creditors of a proprietary concern or a partnership, those of a limited liability company can have no claim against any shareholder except to the extent of the unpaid amount on the shares held by him.

In other words, a limited liability company is a legal entity which is quite separate and distinct from its shareholders and, consequently, creditors do business with the company and must look to it, and not to its members, for payment.

Book Value

The figure of net worth can be used to compute the book value of the various classes of shares. In calculating the book value of a preference share issue, it is treated as an ordinary share issue and the book value is obtained by dividing the net worth by the number of preference shares issued.

From the balance sheet in Exhibit 7, the book or net asset value per share of the 5% Cumulative Tax-free Redeemable First Preference Shares is obtained simply by dividing Rs 3,33,74,384, the amount of net worth, by 10,000 which is the number of shares of this class issued. The book value works out to Rs 3,333.44 per share.

To get the book value per share of the 6 % Second Preference issue, the amount of the capital of the First Preference issue, together with the amount of dividend payable thereon, is deducted from the total of net worth and the balance is divided by the number of Second Preference shares issued. Thus:

	Rs	Rs
Total Net Worth		3,33,74,384
Less: First Preference Share capital	10,00,000	
Add: Accumulated		
dividend for two years	1,30,000	11,30,000
Balance for Second Preference Shares		3,22,44,384
		=========
Number of Second Preference		
Shares issued		30,000
Book Value per Share		Rs 1,074.81

The book value per share of any of the other classes of preference shares can be computed in the same manner. As for equity shares, the book value is obtained by dividing the total of the equity share capital and reserves, the "equity" as this is called, by the number of ordinary or equity shares issued. Using the data in Exhibit 7, this works out to Rs 14.90.

Intangible Assets

While working out the book value per equity share it is customary to deduct the book value of the "intangible assets" from the owners' or shareholders' equity. The figure so obtained is designated the "tangible net worth". The reason for so deducting the book value of the intangibles from total net worth is not that the assets are worthless or unreal, but these are often carried in the books of the company at arbitrary and meaningless amounts.

Besides, such assets depreciate greatly in the event of a dissolution or liquidation. Few companies now-a-days carry intangibles on their balance sheets, however, and those who do, have made it a point to write them off over a period of years by charging a regular amount to the annual profit and loss account as an expense.

From an accounting point of view, an intangible asset is one (1) the value of which is the rights which its possession confers upon the owner, and (2) that does not represent a claim against an individual or business. The principal intangible assets which may appear on the balance sheets of commercial and industrial business concerns are

Brand Names	Goodwill
Copyrights	Leaseholds
Designs	Licences
Drawings	Patents
Formulas	Patterns
Franchises	Processes
	Trade Marks

These intangible assets, which do not possess physical properties but have valuable rights which they confer on the owners, are acquired or developed for use in the regular operations of the business. Their real value is dependent upon their ability to contribute to the earning power of the business. The problem of assigning rupee amounts to them is, therefore, closely related to the valuation of the business as a whole.

It is possible to divide intangible assets into two categories:

1. These having a term of existence limited by law, or agreement, or by their nature. Examples are — copyrights, franchises, leases, licences and patents.
2. Those having no such limited term of existence and at the time of acquisition there is no indication of a limited life. Coming under this category are — goodwill, secret processes, trade marks, technical know how, and the such.

If an intangible asset has a limited legal life, its cost of acquisition or value is frequently written off, as a matter of prudent financial policy, by an annual charge to the profit and loss account during the useful economic life of the asset. But if an intangible asset has no definite useful life, it is for the company possessing it to decide how long the asset should continue to be shown on the balance sheet at its full book value.

If it is felt that the intangible would not continue to have the value during the entire working life of the business, the company may choose to write it off by annual instalments during the estimated useful life of the asset. But, where the intangible is an important income producing factor and is constantly maintained by advertising or in any other way, the company would be justified in showing its full value on the balance sheet.

CHAPTER 7

Long-term Loans and Gearing

To summarise what has been said so far, every company must raise at least some portion of the initial capital required to finance its undertaking from its members or owners. This it does by issuing shares, each of the same specified value, to a legally prescribed number of persons if it chooses to be a private limited company, or to the public at large if it prefers to be a public limited company. The capital so raised is the company's share capital which is permanent in nature and can be repaid only on its dissolution, or reduced under specified circumstances on obtaining the consent of the members and the sanction of a High Court.

When the time comes to undertake a planned expansion of the business by putting up another factory, or to modernise the existing one, the company may need more capital if the build-up of reserves proves inadequate. In this situation, the company may have some thinking to do because it can either raise the required capital or borrow it. The deciding factors in this regard are, (1) the amount of capital funds needed, (2) whether they are to be retained permanently or are to be repayable after some years, (3) the relative ease with which the funds can be obtained in each situation, and (4) the cost of servicing, that is, whether it would be cheaper to raise more share capital or to borrow it.

If the company decides to raise additional permanent share capital it must approach its existing shareholders again and offer to sell them additional shares which normally are of the same class as originally issued. Because they already own the company, the shareholders have the right to accept the offer of new shares so as to maintain thereby their proportionate ownership of the company, or to decline it. For this reason the new shares are called "rights" shares and are offered to each existing shareholder in strict proportion to his current holding at a price which may be equal to or higher than, but rarely less than, the par value of each share.

If a majority of the members, for some reason, are unwilling to accept the fresh offer, the company can, with the consent of the members, offer the shares to the public for subscription through a prospectus as in the case of the original issue. But, if it becomes difficult to sell the shares to the public for any reason such as a.

depressed state of the share market, the company has to think of other ways of raising the required funds. In practice, however, all the different ways of raising capital are considered simultaneously and the one most convenient is selected.

In taking a decision the company not only has to consider the possibility of raising additional share capital either from the existing shareholders or the general public but also the ease and cost of raising the capital.

If the company decides to issue preference or equity shares to the public, it must follow the procedure laid down by law in this regard. It must first secure the consent of the Securities and Exchange Board of India (SEBI) to make a Public Issue. It must also obtain the permission of the existing shareholders in a special meeting to offer the shares to the public. Again, it must advertise the issue in newspapers, print the prospectus and application forms, pay the underwriter's and brokers' commission, send allotment letters and issue share certificates.

All this not only takes time but involves the company in an expenditure which, at times, may be quite large in proportion to the amount of the capital required to be raised. In contrast, it is often simpler and less expensive to approach a bank or a financial institution for a loan if the borrowing limit fixed by law is not exceeded.

Alternatively, the company may raise a loan by issuing debenture bonds to the existing shareholders, or the public, or even to financial institutions. But, here again, the company will have to follow the procedure laid down and bear the expense related to the issue.

Relative Advantages

In addition to the not inconsiderable saving in time, effort and expenses, the company can secure for itself certain other benefits by obtaining a long-term loan from a bank or financial institution.

An issue of equity shares creates a permanent liability for the company as compared to a temporary one created by borrowing. Moreover, if the company makes too many rights or public issues of equity shares not only does its share capital get "diluted" but there arises the possibility of outsiders gaining control of the company through the acquisition or cornering of shares.

If, on the other hand, loans are raised, the creditors will not demand a say in the day-to-day management of the company so long as the interest on the loan advanced by them is paid promptly, or the loan is repaid on the due dates. Besides, from the point of view of the company's liability to pay income tax, it is advantageous to borrow the required capital than to raise it. The interest paid on loans is considered an expense and tends to reduce the liability to pay income tax. In contrast, dividends, whether on preference or equity shares, are a distribution made from profit which is taxable.

Gearing or Leverage

But, the main advantage which an efficiently managed and prospering company can derive by raising a part of the capital by borrowing it at a fixed rate of interest, is the one which flows from the factor known as "gearing", "leverage" or "trading on the equity".

Suppose a company's capital structure, or capitalisation, is made up of debenture bonds, long-term loans from financial institutions, preference shares, equity shares and accumulated reserves.

The interest on long-term loans including debenture bonds, and the dividend on preference shares, by the terms of issue of these securities, are to be paid before any distribution of profits is made to the equity shareholders and hence are called "Senior Charges" so far as earnings for the equity are concerned.

Similarly, the capital raised by taking long-term loans or by issuing debenture bonds and preference shares, is called "Senior Capital". The relative proportion, usually expressed as a percentage, of the senior capital to the total of equity capital and accumulated reserves is known as gearing or leverage. If the proportion is large, the company is said to be high geared; if it is small, the company is said to be low geared.

So long as the cost of servicing the senior capital (interest on debenture bonds plus dividend on preference shares) remains low in comparison with the income earned on the total capital employed, there accrues a definite benefit to the equity share holders because the gearing or leverage acts to enlarge the profit from which dividend to equity shareholders is payable. This can be illustrated by the following example.

A company has an equity share capital of Rs 100 lakh on which it earns a return of thirty per cent or Rs 30 lakh before paying income tax. If the rate of corporate tax is assumed to be forty per cent, the company would be left with a net profit after tax of Rs 1.8 lakh and could pay a maximum dividend of eighteen per cent.

Now suppose that, to take advantage of favourable market conditions the company decides to expand its business by introducing additional capital funds of Rs 100 lakh on which it hopes to earn the same rate of return, that is, thirty per cent. It can either double the equity capital or issue preference shares and debenture bonds in varying proportions. How the method of financing chosen would affect the rate of return on the equity share capital employed is revealed by the following computation:

	Method of Financing		
	A	B	C
	Rs Lakhs	Rs Lakhs	Rs Lakhs
Capital Structure :			
15% Debenture Bonds	100.00	50.00	—
15% Preference Shares	—	50.00	—
Equity Shares of Rs 10	100.00	100.00	200.00
	200.00	200.00	200.00
	=====	=====	=====
Profitability :			
Profit (30% Return on Capital)	60.00	60.00	60.00
Less: Deb. Interest	15.00	7.50	—
Profit before Taxation	45.00	52.50	60.00
Less: Tax @ 40%	18.00	21.00	24.00
Profit after Taxation	27.00	31.50	36.00
Less: Pref. Dividend	—	7.50	—
Net Earned for the Equity	27.00	24.00	36.00
Rate of Return on the Equity Capital (%)	27.00	24.00	18.00
	====	====	====

Thus, under Method C of financing, the rate of return after tax on the equity capital would be the same 18 per cent as it should be, but would be up by one third under Method B and by one-half under Method A.

The reason is simply this that while the newly introduced fixed-interest capital contributes Rs 30 lakh to the profit before taxation, it claims only Rs 15 lakh as debenture interest and preference dividend. A part of the remaining Rs 15 lakh is absorbed by the additional income tax that becomes payable on the enlarged profit while the balance goes to augment the net earnings for the equity.

The explanation for the lesser accretion to net earnings for the equity under Method B than under Method A is that, unlike debenture interest which, for taxation purposes, is a charge against profit, preference dividend is payable out of taxed profits. Hence, under Method B, taxation claims more and leaves a comparatively smaller amount to be added to the earnings for the equity.

Now suppose that as a result of favourable market conditions, the overall profitability of the capital employed jumps to 45 per cent. The result of this on the net earnings for the equity is reflected by the following figures:

	Method of Financing		
	A	B	C
	Rs Lakhs	Rs Lakhs	Rs Lakhs
Profit (45% Return on Capital)	90.00	90.00	90.00
Less: Deb. Interest	15.00	7.50	—
Profit before Taxation	75.00	82.50	90.00
Less: Tax @ 40 %	30.00	33.00	36.00
Profit after Taxation	45.00	49.50	54.00
Less: Pref. Dividend	—	7.50	—
Net Earned for the Equity	45.00	42.00	54.00
Rate of Return on the Equity capital (%)	45.00	42.00	27.00

Thus, while the overall rate of return on the capital employed has enlarged by one-half (from 30 per cent to 45 per cent) that on the equity capital has gone up by as much as two-thirds (from 27 per cent to 45 per cent) under Method A, but no benefit other than the increase of 50 per cent in the overall rate of return, has accrued to the equity holders under Method C, and only a marginally better return under Method B.

Now suppose that the company along with other units in the industry runs into a recession and the rate of return on the capital employed declines by a half to 15 per cent. It could be seen from the following figures that equity holders would suffer the most if Method A of financing was used instead of either Methods B or C. This is because in such a situation the leverage or gearing tends to work in the reverse direction and goes to depress the rate of earning on the equity capital instead of enhancing it.

	Method of Financing		
	A	B	C
	Rs Lakhs	Rs Lakhs	Rs Lakhs
Profit (15 % Return on capital)	30.00	30.00	30.00
Less: Deb. Interest	15.00	7.50	—
Profit before Taxation	15.00	22.50	30.00
Less: Tax @ 40 %	6.00	9.00	12.00
Profit after Taxation	9.00	13.50	18.00
Less: Pref. Dividend	—	7.50	—
Net Earned for the Equity	9.00	6.00	18.00
Rate of Return on the Equity Capital (%)	9.00	6.00	9.00

The foregoing calculations are unrealistic for they ignore the accumulated reserves of the company which represent additional investment by the company on behalf of the shareholders. What is more important is that the company pays no interest to the shareholders for the use of the ploughed back profits which belong to them. There is, therefore, a built-in element of leverage in a capital structure incorporating accumulated reserves and the larger are the reserve the more magnified will be the rate of return on the equity capital employed. Consider the following figures:

	A Ltd. Rs Lakhs	B Ltd. Rs Lakhs	C Ltd. Rs Lakhs
Equity Capital	200	250	300
Reserves	200	150	100
TOTAL EQUITY	400	400	400
Profit before Taxation			
(30 % of Total Equity)	120	120	120
Less: Taxation @ 40 %	48	48	48
Profit after Taxation	72	72	72
Rate of Return on			
Equity Share Capital (%)	36.0	28.8	24.0
Earnings per share of Rs 10	(Rs) 3.60	2.88	2.40

Thus, even though each of the three companies earns the same amount of profit after taxation, the rate of return on the equity capital as well as the earnings per equity share vary because of the difference in the amount of reserves in the capitalisation.

Classification of Loans

On published balance sheets of Indian companies, loans, no matter from which source obtained, are classified as "Secured" and "Unsecured". The former, as their designation suggests, are secured against the mortgage of immovable property and hypothecation of movable property of the borrowing company. The immovable property comprises land, buildings, plant, machinery, equipment and other assets basic to the company's operations. Common items of movable property are stocks of raw materials, components, finished goods and work-in-progress, the book-value of sundry debtors, and investments in subsidiary and associate companies.

Unsecured loans are obtained without providing any such security though repayment is usually guaranteed by one or more directors in their personal capacities. Falling in this category of loans are cash credits, overdrafts and temporary accommodation by banks, loans from directors and others, and fixed deposits from the public.

From the point of view of analysis, however, a more appropriate differentiation between loans is whether they are "current" or "non-current". Current loans, like current liabilities, are returnable within one year from the date of the balance sheet or on demand. Considered as current dues or obligations are cash credits, overdrafts, other loans or accommodations, open mortgages with no fixed maturity, besides annual instalments payable against long-term loans, interest accrued thereon, fixed deposits from the public and cost of plant and machinery purchased on deferred payment basis. Loans other than these are non-current.

Even though loans and borrowings are not classified on the balance sheet the way an analyst would have them grouped, it is not impossible for him to rearrange the published data to meet his requirements.

As stated in Chapter 4, the same balance sheet is read by different interest groups and, as such, must provide the financial information of vital importance to these groups. The law, on the other hand, has its own limitations and can at best prescribe only one or two ways of classifying items of assets and liabilities. But, this does not mean that it is unmindful of the needs of interest groups other than those directly served by the prescribed classification.

Schedule VI to the Companies Act, requires all companies to provide by way of notes to the balance sheet such information as the terms of redemption or conversion (if any) of debentures issued, the nature of the security offered for contracting a loan, the amounts of foreign currency loans and rupee loans repayable within one year from the date of the balance sheet and many other details. An analyst, therefore, is never really starved for information provided he is willing to go through the notes and explanations provided and does not confine himself to reading only the published figures.

Debenture Bonds

While almost all companies raise long-term loans from all-India or State-level financial institutions, the larger ones often raise such loans from the public by issuing debenture bonds. These are secured loans and represent a mortgage on the fixed assets of the issuing companies. They are nothing but certificates issued under the seal of the companies acknowledging the debt and promising repayment of the loan on the expiry of a certain number of years either in full or in instalments.

Debenture bonds carry a fixed rate of interest which is payable, usually every six months, on specified dates whether the issuing company makes a profit or not. They, further, carry the right to legal action should the company fail to pay the promised interest or the principal amount. They appear in the following different varieties although the most common now-a-days are the convertible and non-convertible debentures.

Registered Debentures are those the holders of which are registered in the books of the company. They are, therefore, not freely negotiable and can be transferred from the seller to the buyer only by executing a transfer deed as in the case of preference and equity shares. The interest is paid by post only to the registered holders.

Bearer or Unregistered Debentures are freely negotiable and the title in them can be transferred from the seller to the buyer by mere delivery without giving notice of such transfer to the issuing company. Interest is paid to the holder for the time being or the bearer when he presents the debentures to the company's bank when the payment of interest is due. At times interest coupons are attached to the debenture instrument and the interest amount is paid when they are presented to the issuing company's bankers on due dates. A bearer debenture can be converted into a registered debenture at the holders' option.

Besides being registered and bearer or unregistered, debentures can be redeemable or irredeemable or perpetual. *Redeemable debentures* are repaid or redeemed on a specified date or during a specified period, the principal amount being repayable in one or more instalments. Irredeemable debentures are, obviously, not so repayable and are repayable only on the dissolution of the issuing company. This class of debentures is very rarely issued if at all.

A class of debentures which is becoming increasingly popular with investors and companies wishing to raise loans from the public, is the *Convertible Debenture* which provides the holders the option, subject to specified conditions to exchange the debenture at some future date, for a stated number of equity shares.

CHAPTER 8

Current Liabilities

Moving further down the list of liabilities we come to current liabilities which comprise all those accounts and claims on the company which have to be settled within a relatively short period of time, normally within one year from the date of the balance sheet. While analysing current liabilities it must be remembered that a balance sheet presents a picture of the finances of a company as on only one particular day of the year and even that day may be several months in the past by the time the balance sheet is taken up for study. Meanwhile, the position might have changed, at times radically. Some of the liabilities might have been paid off and new ones might have been contracted and the balance sheet, therefore, might not present the true "current" position.

In the balance sheet of a small proprietary concern, the number of items falling under the head "current liabilities" may be one or two. But, in the case of a large public limited company, the items may be as many as a dozen or more. Common among these are:

(i)   Bank overdrafts and cash credits,
(ii)   Fixed deposits from the public,
(iii)   Instalments due on long-term loans,
(iv)   Notes payable and trade acceptances,
(v)   Sundry creditors for goods and supplies,
(vi)   Accruals,
(vii)   Deposits against orders,
(viii) Advance payments,
(ix)   Unclaimed dividends, and
(x)   Provisions.

Bank Overdrafts and Cash Credits

To augment their working capital, business enterprises frequently obtain over drafts or cash credits from banks. Such temporary loans are often advanced without any security except the personal guarantee of one or more directors. But, at times, these may be secured against the hypothecation of such movable assets as stocks of raw materials or finished goods, work-in-progress, trade debtors and investments in subsidiary and associated companies.

The material point to note is not whether the loan is secured or unsecured but whether or not it is repayable within one year from the date of the balance sheet. If the loan is repayable during the course of the next twelve months it is a current liability. Otherwise, it is a deferred or long-term liability. If no definite redemption or repayment date has been specified, as happens quite often, cash credits and overdrafts are to be treated current fixed liabilities because they may be called back at any time at short notice.

Fixed Deposits from the Public

Many business enterprises these days accept fixed deposits from the public to supplement their working capital. These are necessarily unsecured loans though they are usually guaranteed by two or more directors. When repayable within one year of the date of the balance sheet, they constitute a current liability, otherwise a deferred one.

Instalments Due on Long-term Loans

Borrowings from public financial institutions and loans raised by issuing debenture bonds or convertible notes are, as stated, repayable after some number of years. As such, they are not a current liability.

But at times, repayment is demanded or promised in fixed annual instalments and when this happens to be the case, the annual instalment becomes a current liability. If the entire loan is repayable, like a debenture loan, during a particular year or on a specified date, it becomes a current liability for the year of repayment or redemption.

Notes Payable and Trade Acceptances

Notes payable are "Written promises, signed by the maker, to pay a sum certain in money on demand or at a definite or determinable date in the future". Such promissory notes are issued when goods, merchandise or equipment are purchased on credit and are current liabilities unless the repayment date falls beyond a period of twelve months from the date of the balance sheet.

At times heavy machinery or equipment is purchased on deferred payment terms calling for equal monthly or annual instalments along with accrued interest. Many companies show the full amount of the credit as a current liability which is obviously incorrect. Only the instalment due payable in the current year and the accrued interest thereon are current liabilities and the balance is a deferred or long-term liability.

Sundry Creditors for Goods and Suppliers

These should only include creditors for goods purchased on credit from time to time. Amounts due to partners, officers, shareholders, employees, or subsidiary and associated companies must not be included and should be shown separately.

Accruals

Accruals or accrued liabilities comprise amounts due but not as yet payable as salaries, wages, rent, rates, taxes and interest. A company drawing up its balance sheet as at March 31, is required to pay wages to workers and salaries to staff for the month of March. In most cases these are not paid till the following date or week and so appear on the company's balance sheet as accrued liabilities.

Deposits against Orders

Some companies require their customers to pay a small deposit equal to, say, ten per cent of the value of the goods ordered, at the time of placing the order. Such deposits are treated as initial or part-payments and are adjusted against the total payment due when the order is completed. Thereupon, they automatically disappear from the balance sheet. Till such time, however, as the sale is not consummated, any deposits against orders will have to be treated as temporary loans and hence current liabilities.

Advance Payments

This item arises when part of a sale price is collected in advance, for instance, in the case of newspapers and magazines for subscriptions and advertisements, in the case of insurance companies for premiums, in the case of banks as discounts on bills receivable, and in the case of shipping companies for freight or fares. Such payments constitute a liability till the sale is consummated when they become part of the purchase price.

Unclaimed Dividends

Dividends proposed by the board of directors become payable only when sanctioned by the shareholders at their annual general meeting. Once the dividends are sanctioned, the company takes immediate steps to post the relevant dividend warrants which the shareholders are required to present to the company's bank for payment.

Often, shareholders fail to realise their dividend warrants and so the dividend remains unclaimed and unpaid. Such unclaimed dividends are credited to a special account called "Unclaimed Dividends Account" which appears on the balance sheet as a current liability. The Articles of the Association of companies provide for the forfeiture of dividends which have remained unclaimed for a certain number of years. Such forfeited dividends are then transferred to a special reserve.

Provisions

Provisions are amounts retained, set aside or written off from current profits to provide for a contingency, commitment, liability or diminution in the value of an asset known to exist at the time of the balance sheet but the exact amount of which cannot be determined with sufficient accuracy. Provisions are fully discussed in the next chapter. Suffice it to say for the present that, provisions are current liabilities if the contingency, commitment or liability is going to arise in the course of the next twelve months. The two most common provisions are — (1) Provision for Taxation, and (2) Provision for Dividends.

Summary

A wide divergence is noticed in published balance sheets in the treatment by accountants of items of current liabilities and current assets. For instance, one accountant may treat the instalment of long-term loan payable currently, that is, within the next twelve months as a current liability while another may lump it along with the total long-term loans and indicate the amount repayable during the next financial year in a foot note to the balance sheet. Again one accountant may set up the amount due from an employee as a slow moving asset but another, under similar circumstances, may classify it as a current asset under the omnibus heading "Loans and Advances Recoverable".

Such differences in treatment of individual items of assets and liabilities are due, in some cases, to the differences in the training and experience of the accountants and in some other cases, to management policies and the diversity of purposes for which balance sheets are used. The analyst has the right, however, to reclassify the items according to his understanding and to suit his requirements. The simple rule for him to follow is that any payment due within the following twelve months is a current liability and any payment which reasonably can be expected as receivable is a current asset. Other items are either non-current and deferred or are part of the net worth.

CHAPTER 9

Provisions and What They Are For

The liabilities discussed in the preceding chapter are not only known to exist at the time of preparation of the balance sheet but their exact amounts are also readily ascertainable from the records and books of account of the company. There are certain other liabilities, however, which, too, are known to exist at the time of the balance sheet but the exact amounts thereof are not so ascertainable or are indeterminable. These are commitments such as payment of a declared dividend or contingencies like income tax on the profit earned, which are going to be set up as claims against the company sometime in the near future.

Prudent financial management requires that such commitments or contingencies are adequately provided for and are fully disclosed in the balance sheet of the company along with other liabilities or claims known to exist and are ascertainable. And the only way in which these contingencies can be provided for is to set aside their estimated amounts from the profits of the company, past or present.

It was mentioned in Chapter 6 that profits earned by a company after meeting all expenses of its business are partly distributed as dividends on preference and ordinary shares and are partly retained in the business in the form of reserves. Just now it was said that provisions are also amounts set aside out of profits and other surpluses to meet specific contingencies or commitments. What, then, is the difference between reserves and provisions?

Not infrequently, the terms 'reserve' and 'provision', are regarded as interchangeable and what may appear as a reserve on one balance sheet may be seen as a provision on another. All carefully prepared balance sheets, however, make a clear distinction between reserves and provisions and use the term "reserves" to designate amounts set aside out of profits and other surpluses which are not designed to meet any liability, contingency, commitment, or diminution in the value of an asset known to exist at the time of finalising the accounts at the end of a year.

In contrast, provisions represent amounts written off or retained by way of providing for depreciation, renewals or diminution in the value of assets or retained or set aside to provide for any known liabilities or contingencies the amounts of which cannot be determined with sufficient accuracy.

It follows from this that any amount set aside in excess of the actual requirement is to be treated as a reserve and not as a provision. If, for instance, Rs 5,000 have been set aside to meet a certain liability which, later, is estimated to require only Rs 2,000 the balance Rs 3,000 should be treated as a reserve.

The commitments for which provisions are normally created are:

(i)   Depreciation,
(ii)   Taxation,
(iii) Bad Debts,
(iv)   Gratuity, Pension fund or Retirement Benefits,
(v)   Contingencies,
(vi)   Dividends, and
(vii) Contingent Liabilities.

Depreciation

The land, buildings, plant, machinery and equipment of a company are basic to its operations. They are not normally available for sale but are held permanently for the purpose of production and with a view to earning an income.

When plant and machinery are being used for the purpose of production it is but inevitable that there should be some "wear and tear" of the equipment and the day always comes when the plant and machinery wear out and are no longer capable of production and earnings. At times, a machine may become "obsolete" and need to be replaced by a more modern one.

In either case, the older models must be replaced by newer ones and if no provision has been made during the working life of the machinery, funds may not be available when the time comes for it to be scrapped. It is customary with all good managements, therefore, to set aside from the profits available each year, a portion of the original cost of the various "fixed assets" like land, buildings, plant and machinery for such replacement.

The amount so retained out of the profits is called provision for depreciation or diminution in the value of an asset caused by wear and tear and the passage of time. The balance sheet provides the figure to-date of the depreciation accumulated over the years. But this is not shown separately under the heading "Provisions" and is always deducted from the original cost of assets.

Taxation

A firm or a company is as much liable to pay income tax on the profit earned by it as is an individual on his yearly income. According to the income tax law, the profit of a company is assessable to income tax in the year following the one in which it has been earned.

Besides, the assessable profit may not necessarily be the same as the one shown in the accounts. As such, the income tax payable by the company cannot be correctly ascertained at the time of finalisation of the accounts. An estimate has to be made and the estimated amount is to be set aside out of the available profits as "Provision for Taxation".

The figure appearing on the balance sheet normally comprises (1) the estimated amount of tax payable on the profit earned during the year just completed, and (2) any part still outstanding of the income tax assessed and agreed on the profits of any of the previous years. Anything provided in excess of these amounts is a part of the reserves and is not a provision.

Bad Debts

With the exception of small retail establishments, all large companies sell their goods or services mostly on credit and attempt to recover amounts of the outstanding bills subsequently. It happens that some of the clients find difficulty in meeting their obligations when they are due. The involved amounts then become unrecoverable and have often to be written off as "bad debts".

To prepare themselves to meet this contingency, prudent managements create a "Provision for Bad Debts" by setting aside out of available profits sums equal to the debts likely to be defaulted, or equal to a certain percentage of the total amount due from clients. If the amount becomes unrecoverable it is written off against the provision already made, but if the debt is recovered, the provision becomes unnecessary and is either transferred back to the profit and loss account or to the general reserve.

At times, a reserve instead of a provision for bad debts is created by transferring out of each year's net profit after tax an amount equal to, say, one or two percent of the total outstanding bills. If certain debts become unrealisable they are written off against the reserve and no separate provision is made for the uncollectibles.

Gratuity, Pension Fund or Retirement Benefits

The terms of employment adopted by most well-managed companies provide for the payment, either of a lump-sum gratuity or annual pension or superannuation benefits for a specified number of years to every employee on his retirement from active service with the company. Companies plan to meet this liability in three ways.

Some create a reserve to which credits are made out of the after-tax profits each year and actual payments are debited. Some create a Provision for Gratuity, Pension, etc. and operate it the same way as the reserve above, while some companies neither make a provision nor create a reserve and treat the liability as a contingent liability (see below) and charge actual payments during a year to the profit and loss account as an expense.

It should be clear from what has been said earlier that only the amount of gratuity, pension or terminal benefits payable during the twelve months from the balance sheet date, can truly be called a provision and any excess amount provided is a reserve even though it is designated a provision.

Contingencies

In addition to providing for specific liabilities like depreciation of fixed assets, income tax, bad debts, terminal benefits to employees and dividends to shareholders, companies make provisions for contingencies the nature of which is seldom, if ever, disclosed. Usually, the contingency is a genuine one, such as payment of higher wages or bonus following a Tribunal award awaited or similar claims on the company the precise amounts of which cannot be estimated with accuracy. At times — thankfully rare these days — a provision for contingency may be used as an accounting device to reduce to a more normal level the large profit earned during a highly successful year and to write it back later to bolster those of a lean one.

Dividend

A dividend on equity shares is proposed by the directors but cannot be distributed unless approved by the shareholders in their annual general meeting. But once proposed by the directors it becomes a commitment to be met as soon as approved by the members. This may appear on the balance sheet either as a provision or as a current liability as proposed dividend. But the difference in practice is not really material since in either case the liability is a short-term or current one.

Contingent Liabilities

A contingent liability is a possible future liability which may arise as a result of past circumstances or actions or a possible future event. As of the balance sheet date, there is no actual legal liability of a determinable amount. As such, no specific provision is made in the accounts for such a claim and the fact is merely mentioned in the notes appended to the balance sheet. The more common contingent liabilities are:

1. Claims against the company (for taxes, wages, salaries, etc.) not acknowledged as debts.
2. Amounts of customers' bills of exchange discounted with banks.
3. Uncalled liability on partly paid shares.
4. Arrears of dividends on cumulative preference shares of the company.

CHAPTER 10

Fixed Assets, Depreciation and Cash-Flow

Turning our attention to the assets side of the balance sheets, the first item we come across is "Fixed Assets". These are the land and buildings, plant and machinery, tools and equipment, furniture and fixtures, motor cars and delivery vans, etcetera owned or possessed by a company.

These are called fixed assets because they were so designated by Adam Smith in his "Wealth of Nations" published in 1776. "Some part of capital of every master artificer or manufacturer must be "fixed" in the instrument of his trade", he wrote thoughtfully two centuries ago.

Fixed assets are what a company owns for the purpose of production and are not normally available for sale. They are essentially of a permanent nature and are in constant use to carry on the business of the company. Not every company, of course, owns all the different fixed assets mentioned above.

A bank or an insurance company, for instance, will possess only a building, some motor cars and office furniture and equipment. A large manufacturing company such as the Tata Engineering & Locomotive Company Ltd., on the other hand, will have on its books many types of fixed assets like land, buildings, plant and machinery, tools end equipment, jigs and fixtures, laboratory and testing equipment, electrical installations, railway sidings, motor cars, vans, furniture, patents, trademarks, designs and so on.

Fixed assets are shown in the books of the company at the original cost of purchase less depreciation accumulated over the years. Such "historical" costs usually have little relevance to prevailing market conditions and the assets, therefore, may be overvalued or undervalued.

For instance, land purchased 20 years ago at Rs 10,000 may today be worth Rs 50,000 or more. But since it is shown in the company's books at the original cost, there is a hidden undervaluation to the extent of Rs 40,000. The same will be the case of other assets bought during years when the purchasing power of the rupee was much higher than what it is today.

To get a "true and fair" picture of the financial status of the company it is necessary that fixed assets are revalued at the end of each financial year no matter how vast or complicated such revaluation may prove. There is yet another reason why fixed assets would better be shown in the balance sheet at their current prices instead of their historical costs.

There are some other assets like inventories, sundry debtors and marketable securities which, because of their temporary nature, are shown at current prices and, if historical costs have been used as in the case of investments, their current market prices are also indicated. This means that in the same balance sheet some assets are shown at costs which may have no relevance to prevailing market conditions while there are others which are shown at their present realisable values.

Some accountants oppose any departure from the present practice of showing fixed assets at their historical costs on the ground that a balance sheet is not supposed to reflect economic values but merely values which have been used up in business operations. Besides, frequent reevaluations confuse the records and even if carried out may be purely subjective and may not represent the bargained price for an asset. The Companies Act has noted the objections and has left the matter for voluntary action by the individual boards of directors. The Act, nevertheless, requires that where on a revaluation, the original cost of an asset has been written up or down, the balance sheet must show the date of such revaluation and, further, that each balance sheet for the first five years subsequent to the date of revaluation must show the amount by which the original cost has been written up or down.

Balance sheets of all large commercial or manufacturing companies carry a schedule giving a major classification of fixed assets, their values as at the beginning of the year, additions, retirements sales or transfers made during the year, and the gross or book values as at the end of the year.

Similarly, the accumulated amount of depreciation provided till the end of the previous year, the amount of depreciation provided during the year under review, depreciation on assets sold or transferred, and the amount of depreciation provided to-date are also shown. Finally, the net value after depreciation of each class of assets as at the end of the year under consideration and the one immediately preceding it are stated.

Depreciation

Concept

The basis of depreciation is quite simple. It is the diminution in value caused by the inevitable wear and tear through constant use of such assets as building, plant, machinery, tools, motor vehicles and so on.

No matter how well such assets are maintained or how often they are repaired and renovated, they will one day cease to be as efficient and productive as they once were and will have to be scrapped and replaced. Or, newer and more efficient models may become available and a company may want to replace its existing plant and machinery with them so as to be able to maintain its competitive position in the industry.

It, thus, becomes necessary for every company to set aside each year adequate sums for the eventual replacement of ageing and inefficient assets. If no such sums are set aside, or depreciation allowed for, and the entire profit earned each year is used up for payment of dividends then, when the time comes for the replacement of the worn-out assets, there would be no funds available to purchase new ones.

There has to be, therefore, a "charge for depreciation" each year against profits. The Government, too, has long recognised this legitimate commercial need and accordingly companies are allowed to set aside each year sums, at certain prescribed rates, before their business profits are taxed.

The annual depreciation charge is shown in the profit and loss account as an item of expenditure representing the cost of using the fixed assets during the year. It is not an actual out-go of cash, however, and is in fact a provision which is shown in the balance sheet as a deduction from the value of the fixed assets which appears in the books of the company.

Basic Methods

There are two basic methods used by companies to compute their annual depreciation charge. In the "Straight-line" method a certain fixed percentage of the original cost of assets is written off each year till, as prescribed by the Companies Act, 95 per cent of the cost has been written off at the expiry of the useful life of the assets.

For example, if the cost of purchase of an asset is Rs 1,00,000 and its useful life has been estimated at 10 years, the annual depreciation charge according to the straight-line method will be Rs 9,500 as follows:

$$\text{Annual Depreciation Charge} = \frac{\text{Original Cost} \times 95\%}{\text{Estimated Life (Years)}}$$

$$= \frac{\text{Rs } 1,00,000 \times 95}{10 \times 100}$$

$$= \text{Rs } 9,500$$

The value of the asset in the books of the company will be Rs 90,500 (Rs 1,00,000 Less Depreciation Rs 9,500) at the end of the first year, Rs 81,000 at the end of the second year and so on. After the tenth year, Rs 5,000 will remain as the residual or scrap value of the asset which will be written off to the profit and loss account of the year in which the asset is sold.

It will be noted that under this method of providing depreciation, the same amount is charged to the profit and loss account each year and the cost of the asset less, of course, its scrap value is spread evenly over its useful life.

The second method, "Reducing Balance" or "Written-down Value" is the one used by the Income Tax Department for the purpose of tax computation. In this method, a fixed percentage of the reduced or written-down value of the asset is charged to the profit and loss account every year.

Since the value of the asset goes on diminishing year after year, the annual depreciation charge likewise goes on decreasing. It is highest in the first year and least in the final year of the useful life of the asset which, thereafter, is ready for scrapping.

Suppose that the cost to a company of a machine is Rs 1,00,000 and according to the income tax rules the depreciation permissible is 10 per cent of the depreciated or written-down value per annum. During the year of acquisition of the asset, the depreciation provision will be Rs 10,000.

For the second year, the depreciation provision will be 10 per cent of the written-down value of Rs 90,000 and so is Rs 9,000. For the third year, the written-down value being Rs 81,000 (Rs 90,000 less Rs 9,000) the depreciation charge will be Rs 8,100. It will be observed that in this method the written-down value and the annual depreciation provision both go on diminishing year after year.

There, of course, are other methods of computing depreciation such as the interest method, the production method, and the sales and profit method, but the two most commonly used are the ones described earlier. Of these, again, the straight-line method is commonly preferred by company managements because of its simplicity and ease of application.

Its main drawback, however, is that it does not take into account the fact that, during the earlier years of the life of an asset, the expenditure on repairs and maintenance is less compared with that in the later years when it tends to be heavy. The combined charge for depreciation and repairs and maintenance, therefore, tends to increase with the ageing of the asset.

Under the written-down value method the combined charge is more evenly distributed. Depreciation is heaviest in the earlier years when maintenance requirements are at a minimum, but goes on diminishing rapidly in subsequent years when larger amounts are required to be spent on repairs and maintenance of the assets. Another important difference between the two methods to be noted is that an asset can be written off faster under the straight-line method than in the written-down value method even though the rate of charging depreciation is the same under the two.

Cash-Flow

Concept

As stated, depreciation is not a tangible expense which is paid for by drawing a cheque but is a sum set aside each year, whether there is profit or not, for the replacement of an asset when it is worn-out. Such sums of money can be used to buy new plant or they can be kept in a bank, invested in gilt-edged securities or used in any way that the directors may choose. They, in fact form part of the "cash-flow" which is the amount retained in the business after paying off all expenses including taxes and dividends.

Cash-flow in financial analysis means net income or profit obtained after adding back expense items which currently do not use cash such as depreciation. It may also exclude revenue items which do not currently provide funds. It comes in two varieties — gross and net.

Gross cash-flow is the net profit after tax plus the provision for depreciation. Net cash-flow is obtained from the gross figure by deducting the amount distributed as dividend on preference and ordinary shares. Of the two, net cash-flow is the more important and commonly used because it represents the actual amount of cash retained in the business after all outgoings including dividends.

It is frequently assumed that there will always be a cash-flow at least equal to the provision for depreciation or other adjustments not involving cash. This will be true only if the total revenue (sales and other income) for a period fully covers all of the expenses including depreciation and other write-offs. If the operations for a period result in a loss and if the loss exceeds the "non-cash" adjustments, the cash-flow will be negative instead of being positive. The following table prepared from the profit and loss account of Gammon India Ltd. for the years ended March 31, 1967-72 makes this point clear.

GAMMON INDIA LTD.
Comparative Cash-Flow

Year Ended March 31	Net Profit or Loss Rs '000	Depreciation Rs '000	Cash-Flow Rs '000
1967	998	3,949	4,947
1968	367	3,369	3,736
1969	L 1,317	3,403	2,086
1970	879	3,112	3,991
1971	L 4,854	2,793	N 2,061
1972	L 5,639	2,399	N 3,240

L : Loss. N : Negative.

During three out of the six years, Gammon India Ltd. suffered losses but the loss recorded in 1969 being less than the provision for depreciation, the cash-flow was still positive though nowhere near the 1967 level. The losses suffered in 1971 and 1972, however, exceeded the provision for depreciation for these years and so, the cash-flow for each of the years was negative.

How the Concept Helps

Critics point out that the term cash-flow, meaning net profit inclusive of the provision for depreciation and similar non-cash transactions, is a misnomer since it implies that because of the write-back of expense items like depreciation which do not currently use cash, additional cash has flown into the business when nothing of the sort has really happened. All that has been achieved by adding back to the net profit the provision for depreciation and other non-cash transactions, is to put on a cash basis the annual accounts originally written on the accrual basis.

The critics, nevertheless, admit that cash-flow is a valid analytical tool which, when correctly used, helps explain:

1. How companies are able to finance large-scale expansion or modernisation, or repay heavy borrowings without resorting to fresh equity financing, and
2. Reconcile the difference in the net profit of companies operating within the same industry and otherwise comparable on the basis of their capitalisations, product-mix, and over-all management policies.

The revenue earned by a company from its operations appears on its profit and loss account for the year as "Sales and Other Income". After deducting from this the expenses of the business including depreciation and income tax, there is left a balance commonly termed the net profit (or loss) for the year.

But, unlike the out of pocket expenses like raw material costs, salaries, wages, etcetera, depreciation and similar provisions do not represent current outlays of cash. To arrive at the true spending power generated through operation it is necessary to add back to the net profit the items which do not constitute either a source or a disposition of cash such as depreciation which is one of the heaviest "expense" items listed on the profit and loss account.

Illustration – Problem 1

During the year ended September 30, 1964, Indian Oxygen Ltd. embarked on a programme of substantial expansion of capacities to be completed in four years and requiring an outlay of Rs 600 lakh. The project was to be financed by a loan of 500,000 pound sterlings from the parent company, British Oxygen Company Ltd., a mid-term bank loan of Rs 200 lakh, and funds generated internally from operations.

By September 30, 1967, new assets worth Rs 513 lakh had been acquired and long-term loans had increased to Rs 294 lakh. The expansion programme was completed, as planned, a year later when fresh capital expenditure of Rs 90 lakh was incurred bringing the total amount spent on the project since its commencement to Rs 603 lakh.

Long-term loans had, by then, started to decline and continued to decrease till they were reduced to Rs 72 lakh by September 30, 1972. These declined further as the mid-term bank loan of Rs 200 lakh was fully repaid and a further instalment was paid to British Oxygen Company Ltd.

During the nine-year period from October 1, 1963 to September 30, 1972, the share capital of Indian Oxygen Ltd. remained unchanged at Rs 462 lakh and the total addition to reserves was Rs 234 lakh excluding the revaluation reserve of Rs 110 lakh. The total amount of depreciation charged to profits during the period was Rs 695 lakh or, in other words, more than enough to cover fully the cost of expansion and to repay long-term loans without having to raise additional share capital.

Illustration – Problem 2

The second situation leading to the development of the cash-flow concept is the wide divergence in accounting practices within specified industries, especially depreciation accounting. As said earlier, the Companies Act allows companies a wide choice in the matter of selection of the method of computation of the annual depreciation charge.

Since it is not necessary that two companies operating within the same industry will adopt the same method of depreciating their fixed assets, the latitude allowed by the Companies Act inevitably leads to a wide variation in the "net" profit earned during the same accounting period by companies otherwise comparable.

Suppose two companies, A and B, both earn a profit of Rs 50,00,000 for a particular year before providing for depreciation and taxation. Company A uses the written-down value method to provide for depreciation of its fixed assets and charges Rs 20,00,000 to the year's profit as depreciation. Company B uses the straight-line method and provides Rs 16,00,000. Each company provides Rs 18,00,000 for taxation after taking into account depreciation computed at income tax rates. The net profit after tax of Company B will be shown in the published accounts Rs 4,00,000 larger than the net profit of company A as follows:

	Company A Rs	Company B Rs
Profit before Depreciation and Taxation	50,00,000	50,00,000
Less – Depreciation	20,00,000	16,00,000
Profit before Tax	30,00,000	34,00,000
Less – Tax	18,00,000	18,00,000
Profit after Tax	12,00,000	16,00,000

This difference would be ironed out, however, if the cash-flow figure were to be used instead of the net profit figure for comparing the performance of the two companies as would be seen from the following computation:

	Company A Rs	Company B Rs
Net Profit after Tax	12,00,000	16,00,000
Add: Depreciation	20,00,000	16,00,000
Cash-flow	32,00,000	32,00,000

Published Accounts

It is now mandatory for Indian companies whose shares and debenture bonds are listed on recognised stock exchanges, as well as for large commercial, industrial and business enterprises in the public and private sectors, to publish along with their annual accounts, a statement showing changes in the financial position of the companies during the period covered by the profit and loss account for the period just ended and the corresponding previous period.

Although invariably designated "cash-flow statement" it is, in fact, a Funds Statement or a Statement of Changes in Financial Position — a title recommended by Accounting Standard 3 (AS 3) issued by the Council of the Institute of Chartered Accountants of India.

The statement comes in three parts - the first showing cash-flow from operating activities, the second the cash-flow from investing activities and the third the cash-flow from financing activities. Each part ends with a figure showing the net amount of cash received from or used in operations or activities. The statement as a whole provides the figure of the net increase or decrease in cash and cash equivalents. This, of course, is tallied with the figure provided by the balance sheet.

CHAPTER 11

Miscellaneous Assets

Miscellaneous assets, to borrow a simile, are "Like odd pieces of furniture that go to furnish a house, not absolutely essential so far as livability is concerned, but necessary to round out the picture". They are not intangible, of course, but appear more commonly on balance sheets of large companies and seldom, if ever on those of medium-sized concerns. They are less permanent in nature than fixed assets but are not as much circulating as are current assets. More common among such assets are:

1. Dues from partners, directors, officers and employees
2. Investments
3. Investments in and amounts due from subsidiary and associated companies
4. Miscellaneous expenditure not written off, and
5. Profit and loss account deficit.

Dues from Partners, Directors, Officers and Employees

Loans are frequently advanced to partners, directors, officers and employees to meet heavy unexpected expenses or to purchase residential accommodation, motor cars or other means of transport, household furniture and similar durable goods. The loans are recovered in monthly instalments from the salary or wages of the incumbents.

More often than not, such advances are lumped with other commercial advances or prepaid expenses and are shown under the heading "Loans and Advances in Cash or in Kind for Value to be Received". Although never too large, these amounts should be segregated from prepaid expenses or other loans made for purely business purposes and shown separately as slow-moving miscellaneous assets.

Investments

Investments is a puzzling item in a balance sheet. Always shown between Fixed Assets and Current Assets, they may represent investment of cash not immediately required for current operations, securities of a speculative nature, or securities which may either be not tradeable or just worthless. Again, they may represent money sunk in some other business or in property that has nothing to do with the conduct of the main enterprise, or securities of subsidiary and associated companies.

All properly drawn balance sheets provide full particulars of investments in:

1. Government or Trustee securities
2. Stocks and shares of companies with a further breakdown into
   (i)   Partly and fully paid shares of different classes,
   (ii) Shares of companies not under the same management, and
   (iii) Shares of subsidiary companies.
3. Immovable properties.

Investments are classified as quoted and unquoted and, for the former, the market valuation as at the date of the balance sheet is given.

Temporary investments represent the investment of cash not required currently for the operations of the business and belong to the current assets section of the balance sheet. They may include:

1. Time deposits with banks.
2. Government and Trustee securities.
3. Stocks and shares of companies not under the same management if readily marketable, and
4. Other investments which can be converted into cash at short notice.

To be properly classified as "temporary", investments (1) must represent a short-term investment of cash with the intention of reconversion when the cash is needed for current operations or emergencies, and (2) must be readily marketable at an approximately definite price. The two major characteristics of temporary investments, therefore, are marketability and availability for use in paying current liabilities.

The following should not be included as temporary investments among current assets of a business

1. Stocks and bonds of subsidiary and associated companies unless they can be, and will be converted into cash which will be used for current operations.
2. Securities which are earmarked for specific funds such as pension fund, retirement gratuity fund, or debenture redemption fund.
3. Securities of uncertain value, and
4. Securities which are not readily marketable.

An investment of any of the above types is to be shown in the fixed assets or miscellaneous assets section of the balance sheet.

Investments in and Amounts due from Subsidiary and Associate Companies

One company is said to be a subsidiary of another if more than fifty per cent of its equity share capital is held by the other company which, then, is called the "Holding Company" or the "Parent Company" of the first company. A subsidiary is wholly-owned if its entire share capital is held by the parent company. It is partly-owned if only a part — but always more than one-half of the share capital is held by the parent and the balance by outside shareholders.

If the interest of one company in another is exactly fifty per cent or less, the second company is said to be an associate or an affiliate of the first. The balance of the share capital of the associate may be held by another company or by hundreds of shareholders and may even be listed on the stock exchanges.

Investments in shares and bonds of associate and subsidiary companies are called "Trade Investments". Since holding such investments depends on the trading policy of the investing company, they are more-or-less permanent in nature and, for that reason, are to be treated as fixed assets or long-term assets and never as current assets like temporary investments.

Similarly, amounts advanced to a subsidiary to help it tide over a temporary difficulty, is either a slow moving miscellaneous asset or a current asset depending upon whether the loan is recoverable in the near future or has already frozen because of the continuing financial difficulties of the subsidiary. To ascertain the current position it becomes necessary to obtain a breakdown of the amounts advanced to subsidiaries and associated companies and an explanation regarding the terms on which each loan has been advanced. In cases where such an explanation is not available it is prudent to treat the entire amount a slow-moving miscellaneous asset.

Miscellaneous Expenditure

Miscellaneous expenditure represents expense items of a non-recurring nature and not arising out of the current operations of the business. They are usually written off against profits in annual instalments over a period of years. Such expenditure includes:

1. Preliminary or formation expenses
2. Expenses including commission or brokerage on or subscription of shares or debentures
3. Discount allowed on issue of shares or debentures
4. Interest paid out of capital during a period of construction

5. Development expenditure not adjusted, and
6. Other items.

All such items, in reality, are of an intangible nature and should be written off against the reserves or the net worth.

Profit and Loss Account — Deficit

Sometimes accumulated deficit to the profit and loss account appears at the end of the assets side of the balance sheet end continues to appear till absorbed in future profits. Like miscellaneous expenditure, such a deficit is also an intangible asset and should be written off from the net worth whenever it appears.

CHAPTER 12

Current Assets, Loans and Advances

There are two categories of assets which every company owns. The first comprises fixed assets and trade investments which are basic to its operations and which are used to manufacture or procure the different products it sells or to provide the services it renders. These assets are employed continuously and are discarded only when they cease to be useful or become obsolete or worthless.

The second equally important category is current assets. Essentially, these are cash, readily marketable securities, and physical assets like stocks of raw materials and finished goods, and work-in-progress which are going to be turned into cash within a comparatively short time. This is why they are called current assets. They are the "constantly changing currency of the business" and are usually listed on the balance sheet in the reverse order of the ease with which they can be converted into cash.

Whether an asset is current or fixed depends upon the function it is expected to perform. A fleet of trucks will represent a current asset to a manufacturer of commercial vehicles since he is going to sell it presumably for a profit. But it will be a fixed asset for a road transport operator who is going to use it, so long as it remains serviceable, to earn an income.

Similarly, a lathe may be a current asset for a machine tool maker or dealer but with most engineering workshops it is a fixed asset. Thus, it is the purpose behind the asset, and not its nature, which decides whether it is current or fixed.

Current assets are of two types — (1) Circulating, (2) Liquid. Circulating assets are those which are produced in the course of business and are held only temporarily till sold and are ultimately converted into cash which may be used to purchase fresh assets which themselves may be encashed and so on. In other words, they are continuously circulating, that is, going out in one form and returning in another, over and over again.

Liquid assets, on the other hand, are those which are readily available to meet immediate liabilities or contingencies and include cash at bank or in hand, and short-term investments. Circulating assets comprise stocks of raw materials, work-in-progress and finished goods, and trade debtors.

Heading the list of current assets on Indian balance sheets is interest accrued on investment but not yet received. Except in the case of investment trusts, holding companies and trading companies, this item is seldom large and of any material significance. It is followed by four distinct groups of current assets — (1) Stocks, (2) Debtors, (3) Cash, and (4) Loans and Advances, in that order.

1. Stocks

Stocks or inventories are the physical part of current assets and so far as published balance sheets are concerned, include stocks of raw materials, stores, spare parts and tools, work-in-progress, that is, semi-finished goods, finished goods ready for sale or despatch, and goods-in-transit or goods which have been sold but have not yet reached the customers.

Inventories is the largest and most important item among current assets on most balance sheets of both large and small concerns, and the management has limitless opportunities to manipulate the value of closing stocks and to inflate or deflate it with a view to presenting a picture quite different from the one which actually exists.

The law, no doubt, requires the management to certify the value of closing stocks and also to state the mode of valuation. But, there is no independent check either on the physical quantity of stocks or their valuation and the management's certification is generally accepted.

All well-managed and forward-looking enterprises, however, keep careful records of all in-coming and out-going stocks and take a physical count of the inventory of stocks at least once every year, while the more progressive among them have adopted a "perpetual inventory system" under which a continuous record is kept of the movement of every item of stock.

Various methods have been devised and used for the valuation of inventories but the one most commonly employed in this country is "Actual cost or market value whichever is lower". The average cost of purchase of a unit of stock is compared with the ruling market price and the lower of the two is accepted for valuation.

The practical business theory behind this method is that, in those cases where the market price is higher than the cost, profit should not be anticipated and the lower actual cost should be taken as the basis for valuation. But, if the market price is lower than the cost, the probable loss, though not actually incurred, should be anticipated and the lower market rate should be taken for the purpose of valuation.

At times a company pays a deposit or advance against its order for supplies of raw materials or other items of stores. This may be viewed as money owed to the company and is shown under the last heading "Loans and Advances".

Almost always, stocks of stores, supplies, spare parts and loose tools are shown as current assets along with stocks of raw materials and finished goods. Such items should be distinguished from inventories of raw materials and work-in-progress because, although essential to production and the general operations of the factory, such items do not become a measurable integral part of the finished goods. Besides, their consumption is only gradual and never as rapid as that of raw materials or components. And finally, such stocks often include redundant or non-usable items which, for one reason or another, have not been written off.

It is prudent, therefore, that stocks of office supplies, spare parts and loose tools are not considered as current assets at all and are included among miscellaneous slow-moving assets. Inventories should include only: (1) stocks of raw materials and components which are currently to be consumed in the production of goods or services to be available for sale, (2) work-in-progress or goods in the process of manufacture, (3) Goods ready for sale in the ordinary course of business, and (4) Goods-in-transit where the title to the goods has passed to the purchaser.

2. Sundry Debtors

The second category of current assets is "Debtors" or "Sundry Debtors" and represents amounts due to a company by its customers for goods sold to them on credit. The book-value of sundry debtors must not include amounts due for the sale of machinery or non-usable items of stocks, amounts due from directors, officers and employees, and amounts due from subsidiary and associate companies. These "miscellaneous" receivables do not arise in the ordinary course of business and will not be collected in accordance with the normal credit terms.

The law requires that particulars be given separately of:

1. Debts considered good and in respect of which the company is fully secured,
2. Debts considered good but for which the company holds no security other than the debtor's personal security,
3. Debts considered doubtful or bad.

Again, debts outstanding for more than six months are to be segregated from other loans and shown separately in the balance sheet.

It is a prudent practice to create a reserve or provision for doubtful debts but, too often, the practice is not followed and if any debts become unrecoverable they are treated as an item of expenditure and written off to the profit and loss account. Where a reserve or a provision for bad or doubtful debts has been created, it should be deducted from sundry debtors for the purpose of analysis.

Sundry debtors are current assets only when they represent amounts receivable for goods sold or services rendered in the normal course of everyday business. Amounts due for sale of non-current assets or due from officers or other employees are not current assets in the strictest sense of the term. These are usually shown separately under the heading "Loans and Advances".

It is clear that, when loans advanced to officers and employees are recoverable through instalments spread over a number of years, only such amounts as are receivable during the next twelve months are current assets, the balance is a deferred or slow moving asset.

At times, sundry debtors include amounts due from subsidiary and affiliate companies or from companies under the same management. Such items should be carefully scrutinised and investigated. The item may represent sales made on normal terms which are met promptly on those terms, or the subsidiary or affiliate may be in an extended financial condition and, because of the community interest, it may be difficult for the parent or holding company to press for payment. In a situation of this sort the amount may, at best, represent a temporarily frozen asset to be included among miscellaneous slow-moving assets.

3. Temporary Investments

The third category of current assets is cash and invested cash. The term "invested cash" embraces several types of investments. Money in excess of normal requirement may be invested, with a view to earning an income, in equity or preference shares and/or debentures bonds listed on the stock exchanges, or in Government securities quoted or unquoted. Investments in subsidiary and affiliate companies are rarely sold and are held permanently as a matter of business policy.

These, as we have seen, form part of the fixed assets of the company and are basic to its operations. Similarly, investments in shares or bonds of companies belonging to the same group or under the same management are held as long as possible and are sold only when absolutely necessary. Such investments do not form part of invested cash and should be treated either as fixed assets or slow-moving miscellaneous assets.

Invested cash, therefore, represents only those investments which are (1) a short-term deployment of cash with the intention of reconversion when the cash is needed for current operations or emergencies, and (2) are readily marketable at an approximately definite price. Such temporary investments may include (i) time deposits in banks, (ii) marketable securities, (iii) other readily marketable investments.

Marketable securities should not include, however, (1) stocks and bonds of subsidiary and affiliate companies or of companies under the same management, (2) securities which are earmarked for specified funds such as retirement fund, gratuity fund or a pension fund, (3) securities of uncertain value, and (4) securities not readily marketable.

Temporary investments are shown on balance sheets at cost with a notation relating to their current market values. If the market value is lower than the cost, conservative analysis requires that the lower market value should be accepted to recognise a potential loss and the difference between the higher cost and the lower market value be deducted from the reserves or the net worth.

Cash

Cash consists of cash in hand and in savings and current accounts with banks *as* also of legal tender like cheques, drafts and postal orders. It must not include post-dated or dishonoured cheques, time deposit certificates and postage stamps.

At times unrestricted cash available for normal operations may include amounts earmarked for specific purposes such as repeating redeemable preference shares or maturing debenture bonds, or cash set aside for the expansion, modernisation or renovation of a factory continuation. Such "restricted" cash should be segregated from cash freely available and shown among slow moving miscellaneous assets.

Similarly, cash in a frozen account in a domestic or foreign bank is not a current asset since it is not freely available. Prior to the country's partition many companies having their head-offices in India, owned tea gardens in the Sylhet district of what was once East Pakistan and is now Bangladesh. For several years after partition, the ownership of the tea gardens continued to be vested in Indian companies but the proceeds from the sale of tea by such gardens were not allowed to be repatriated to India.

The result was that substantial amounts of cash legally belonging to Indian companies accumulated in banks in Pakistan. Although such amounts appeared as freely available cash on the balance sheets of the Indian companies, they were, as a matter of fact, slow-moving assets which should have been separated from the current assets.

How much ready cash a company should hold depends on particular circumstances and the nature of the company's business. If a company has a long cycle of operations, that is, if its products take a long time to make, then it might need more spare cash than another whose goods are flowing faster through the factory line and are being rapidly delivered.

But, whatever the amount of cash held, it must be sufficient to defray promptly the normal expenses of the business. Any excess amount held over and above the absolute minimum, as a general thing, places a concern in an improved financial position.

The importance of cash may be overemphasised at times and a company may hold cash far in excess of its normal requirements. If a firm is doing brisk and profitable business, if it has a good standing with its banks and has a firm grip on its debtors, then the possession of a large balance is not necessary. Too much of idle cash is a wastage of costly capital even if it is temporarily invested in readily marketable securities.

4. Loans and Advances

The last and final category of current assets on Indian balance sheets is "Loans and Advances". This includes, according to the Companies Act:

1. Advances and loans to subsidiaries/partnership firms in which the company or any of its subsidiaries is a partner,
2. Bill of exchange held,
3. Advances recoverable in cash or kind for value to be received, that is, Rates, Taxes, Insurance Premia and the such,
4. Balance with Customs, Port Trust and other government agencies (where payable on demand).

Advances and Loans to Subsidiaries

It has already been explained why advances and loans to subsidiary and affiliate companies should not be treated as current assets but as slow-moving miscellaneous assets. While trying to analyse this item, it is necessary to obtain particulars of the amounts due from each subsidiary and affiliate and an explanation of how each advance or loan arose. After getting the necessary details it should be decided whether the amount represents a loan likely to be repaid in the near future or has already become frozen and unrecoverable.

Bills of Exchange

A bill of exchange is "an unconditional order in writing addressed by one person to another, signed by the person giving it, requiring the person to whom it has been addressed to pay on demand or at a fixed or determinable future time, a sum certain in money to order or to bearer".

In trade or industry, a bill of exchange is drawn upon a customer for goods sold and is accepted by him at the same time the sale is made. The bill is accepted by the customer if he does not wish to pay cash and take advantage of the credit facility offered by the seller.

Generally, there are three conditions under which a bill of exchange materialises (1) when the buyer wants extra terms which are longer than those normally allowed in the trade or by the seller, (2) if the buyer is weak financially and the seller wishes to have a written evidence of the credit allowed, and (3) to provide a written acknowledgement of a past account or loan due.

If the total of bills of exchange receivable includes any amount due from subsidiary or associate companies, directors, officers or employees, it should be segregated and shown under slow-moving miscellaneous assets.

It is not unusual to come across a balance sheet with a foot-note showing a contingent liability for customers' bills of exchange discounted with a bank. In a situation of this sort, the analyst should add back the amount of bills discounted to the total of bills receivable shown under current assets and add a corresponding amount to the balance due to banks appearing under current liabilities. Unless this is done, the balance sheet will not have been put on a comparative basis and a year-to-year comparison of current assets and current liabilities will not be possible.

Advances Recoverable in Cash or Kind

This is an omnibus figure made up of a number of small items such as prepaid expenses, loans and advances to partners, directors, officers or employees, and subsidiary and associate companies, advance payment of tax and so on.

Prepaid Expenses represent the balance or amounts paid for services or for such items as rent, rates, taxes, insurance premia, magazine subscriptions, not received or the benefit of which had not been fully realised as at the date of the balance sheet. Such balances are carried over and are charged to the profit and loss account for the following year.

To give an illustration, a company which ends its accounting year on March 31, pays on January 1, Rs 144 as annual subscription for a certain journal. Of this amount, Rs 36 represent an expense for the year ending on March 31 and the balance will be consumed in the following year. It is, therefore, shown as a current asset in the balance sheet as at March 31 of the year of payment.

As said, loans and advances to partners, directors, officers, employees, or to subsidiary and affiliated companies, should not be treated as current assets but as slow-moving assets.

Treatment of advance payment of income tax differs from company to company. Some show it as a current asset, others show it as a deduction from the provision for taxation under current liabilities. Since the amount of advance payment is related to the estimated tax liability for the current year and may vary from year to year, it may be advantageous to list it under current assets than be shown as a deduction from the provision for taxation.

Deposits with Government Agencies

Companies are often required to maintain a certain balance as deposit with government agencies such as the customs, port trusts and similar bodies. If such balances are returnable on demand, they constitute a current asset otherwise a slow-moving asset.

Summary

As in the case of current liabilities, opinion regarding whether an asset is current or non-current varies from person to person. The common sense rule that only an asset realisable in cash within one year from the date of the balance sheet is to be reckoned as current proves useful, no doubt. But, borderline cases will still be met with and correct classification may prove difficult.

In such situations the analyst should follow the conservative principle that whereas a liability can be assumed as current, an asset, under similar circumstances, should never be until realised. To put it differently, current liabilities can be overstated but current assets must never be.

CHAPTER 13

Working Capital and Its Importance

Over and above the capital invested in fixed assets, a company requires finance for the day-to-day running of its business. It has to carry all the time, adequate stock of raw materials and supplies required for manufacture, and of finished goods and merchandise for sale. In addition, it has to provide credit to its customers on the best possible terms and must have ready cash to defray immediate expenses.

The finance so invested is the company's (gross) working capital and is represented by its current assets. This is one definition of working capital and appeals to the businessman and economist both of whom are concerned only with the amount of finance available and not with the various sources from which it has been obtained.

When so defined, working capital is sometimes referred to as "operating capital" because it supports the day-to-day operations of the company. Or, it may be designated "circulating capital", a term which emphasises the fact that the different current assets circulate or change form frequently during a year from cash to raw materials to inventories to sundry debtors; and back to cash. The definition is quantitative since it refers to the total amount of funds used for operating purpose but ignores their source.

The creditor, the accountant and the investment analyst take a different view, however, and define working capital as the excess of current assets over current liabilities, that is, only that portion of current assets financed by owners or shareholders and long-term creditors such as bond-holders.

This interpretation of working capital is qualitative in substance since it distinguishes or differentiates between the various sources from which finance has been or can be obtained. Besides, it serves as an index of the financial soundness of the business and the margin of protection available to current creditors. When defined in this manner, working capital, obviously, cannot be increased by obtaining short-term loans from banks and others, or by securing an extension of credit from suppliers of goods and services.

To distinguish between these two concepts of working capital, it is now customary to designate total current assets as "working capital" and to apply the term "net working capital" to the excess of current assets over current liabilities or what is shown on some balance sheets as "net current assets".

When a business is started, the capital provided by the owners and obtained as long-term loans, ought to be sufficient to cover, in the first place, the amount sunk in fixed assets and then there should be a further sum available to finance trading. Such an amount is the original working capital of the business and, if things go as well as anticipated, not only does it remain intact but increases over the years as profits are ploughed back to support on expanding volume of sales. The initial amount as increased by a regular plough-back of profits, represents the normal, permanent, or regular working capital, that is, the irreducible minimum of current assets required to conduct business even during relatively dull periods.

The volume of business or trading which can safely be undertaken depends upon the amount of working capital available. If it is desired to increase the volume of business, additional working capital becomes necessary and can be introduced by raising additional share capital or long-term loans or by obtaining more short-term credit from banks and suppliers. But, since none of these sources can supply unlimited finance, there is an obvious upper limit to the working capital.

When the volume and course of business both remain steady, the amount of working capital required will fluctuate within well-defined limits. But, when the business is subject to seasonal or cyclical fluctuations, the amount of working capital needed will run up very high in some months of the year than in others.

Businesses subject to seasonal fluctuations — manufacture of woollen garments, for example — commence their manufacturing or processing activities some months before the start of the season. Their requirement of working capital then reaches its peak because more finance or credit is required to purchase raw materials, pay wages, defray incidental expenses and build up stocks of finished goods. At the end of the season when inventories have been fully or largely liquidated, the working capital reaches its lowest level.

The working capital of businesses subject to seasonal fluctuations can, therefore, be divided into two parts — (1) a more-or-less fixed and permanent amount equal to the minimum of current assets (mostly cash and temporary marketable investments) that have to be carried during the period of least business activity, and (2) a variable amount of current assets (cash, sundry debtors and inventories) the amount of which depends upon the level of seasonal activity anticipated.

In the case of a business subject to cyclical fluctuations, the amount of working capital required depends on the stages of the business cycle. In periods of depression when the business volume declines, the business is left with excess of cash which may be accumulated, used to purchase marketable securities, or pay creditors, or consumed if the business is being operated at a loss. In periods of prosperity when business activity expands larger amounts of cash and credit are required to build up adequate stocks of raw materials, finished goods and/or merchandise.

Normally, a larger proportionate part, if not all, of the more regular or permanent working capital should be provided by the owners of the business either in the form of share capital or ploughed-back profits and the larger such part is ' the better will be the credit rating of the business. The remaining portion may be obtained from long-term creditors such as debentureholders, commercial banks or specialised financial institutions.

Among the commonest sources of seasonal or temporary working capital are bank overdrafts or cash credits, loans from directors, employees, and shareholders, fixed deposits from the public and suppliers of raw and other materials. It must be noted, however that such credits do not change the amount of "net" working capital because both current liabilities and current assets are increased by the same amount.

It is elementary that every company must have adequate working capital at all times if it is to run its business smoothly and economically, if it is to meet its obligations promptly and if it is to meet emergencies and losses without the fear of a total financial collapse. But, whether the available working capital is adequate or not will be determined by several factors and cannot be the same for the different types and sizes of businesses.

The factors which come into play are (1) the time required to obtain or manufacture the goods meant for sale, (2) the value of goods to be sold, (3) the volume of sales, (4) the terms on which goods and services are sold, (5) the duration of the operating or manufacturing cycle, (6) the speed with which finished goods or merchandise can be sold, (7) the terms of credit allowed to customers and how quickly they settle their accounts, and (8) the business cycle and seasonal variations.

An initially adequate working capital may later prove inadequate because of several factors acting singly or in combination. These factors include (1) continuous operating losses, (2) large non-operating losses, (3) the inability of the management to obtain from other sources funds needed to finance an expanding business, (4) an unwise or over-liberal dividend pay-out policy which may prompt payment of dividends, wholly or partly, out of accumulated reserves, (5) excessive investment in non-current assets especially fixed assets, and (6) increasing prices which may require a larger amount to be invested to maintain the same physical quantity of raw materials, and finished goods.

Excessive working capital especially in the form of cash or temporary marketable investments, will be just as unfavourable to a business as an inadequate working capital because of large amounts of funds not being used profitably or productively. It has been observed that idle funds not only involve a company in loss of interest and other income but lead to carelessness about costs and general inefficiency in operations.

The situation may be the result of (1) the issuance of capital or debenture bonds or raising long-term loans in amounts larger than necessary for the acquisition of fixed and non-current assets, (2) the sale of fixed assets which are not later replaced, and (3) large plough-backs of operating profits not used for payment of dividends, acquisition of assets or business expansion.

CHAPTER 14
Profit and Loss Account

The third and the final part of the annual report of a commercial or an industrial business enterprise is made up of the profit and loss account, the first two parts being respectively the directors' and auditors' report to the shareholders, and the balance sheet with its attached schedules and annexures.

To quote an authority, the profit and loss account is the "mathematical interpretation of the policies, experience, knowledge and aggressiveness of the management of the business enterprise from the point of view of income, expenses, gross profit, operating profit, and final net profit or loss".

In essence the profit and loss account is a schedule which sets out the income from and expenses of running a business over a period of time, usually one year, and then gives a final figure representing the amount of profit earned or the loss sustained.

Whenever the tabular or horizontal form of presenting the profit and loss account is adopted, the various sources from which income has been earned are, by tradition, listed on the right-hand side, and the several expense items on the left-hand side as shown in Exhibit 8. This form has gone almost out of fashion now and most companies have adopted the statement or vertical form shown in Exhibits 9 and 10.

The Companies Act does not prescribe the form in which the profit and loss account must be presented but only states that whatever information is being supplied should be sufficient to present a true and fair picture of the operations of the company during the period to which the accounts relate.

Part II of Schedule VI of the Companies Act provides that the profit and loss account should disclose (1) the results of working of the company during the period covered by it and that (2) every material feature including credits or receipts and debits or expenses in respect of non-recurring transactions or transactions of an exceptional nature.

Further, the profit and loss account shall set out the various items relating to the income and expenditure of the company arranged under the most convenient heads. The profit and loss account shall also show the specific information required under paragraphs 3, 4, 4A and 4B of the Schedule and, for each item, the corresponding figure for the previous year shall also be provided.

As a result of these requirements of the law, published accounts of almost all limited liability companies have attained a high degree of uniformity although it cannot be said that the form of presentation usually adopted is best suited to meet the requirements of the analyst as would be seen from Exhibit 9 and its variation Exhibit 10.

Multiple-step Form

In either case the profit and loss account has been presented as a "single step" statement showing the income earned from sales (or trading) and other sources, the various expense items grouped according to their type or nature (raw material costs, staff costs, other expenses, interest, etcetera), the profit earned before and after providing for income tax, and the appropriation of the latter to reserves and dividend payments.

Since the expense items have not been classified according to the functions or departments such as manufacturing, selling, administration and overall management, it is not possible to work out the profit earned at successive stages of operation of the business. To be truly informative and complete, the profit and loss account needs to be split into four distinct parts, namely,

Manufacturing Account to show the cost of manufacture of goods for sale or the cost of sales.

Trading or Operating Account showing the expenses incurred in selling the goods manufactured.

Profit and Loss Account showing the profit earned after allowing for overall administrative, financial and general expenses.

Profit and Loss Appropriation Account showing how the net profit after taxation has been allocated to different reserves and purposes.

The advantage of showing the profit and loss account split into four parts as above is that, the profitability and efficiency of each department is brought to light. When this scheme is adopted it obviously becomes necessary to apportion, on some equitable basis, common items of expenditure such as salaries, wages and employee benefits; rent, rates, taxes and insurance; depreciation; repairs and maintenance; water and electricity; printing and stationery, and so on.

The schedule in Exhibit 11 extracted from the annual report of an Indian subsidiary of a multinational company, shows how some forward looking companies do take the trouble to make their financial statements more enlightening (figures have been omitted for the sake of convenience).

If, for some reason, it is not possible to split the profit and loss account into four distinct parts as suggested, the different items of income and expenditure should be so grouped and allocated to

Exhibit 8   **Profit & Loss Account for the Year Ended March 31, 20__**

	Schedule	20__ (Rs)	20__ (Rs)
Opening Stock:			
Finished Goods			
Materials in Process			
Raw Materials consumed			
Purchase of Finished Goods			
Cotton, Staple Fibre, Rayon, Salt Expenses, etc.	1		
Manufacturing Expenses	2		
Payment to and Provision for Employees			
Sundry Expenses	3		
Director's Fees and Travelling Expenses	4		
Depreciation			
Investment Allowance Reserve			
Provision for Taxation			
Balance, being Profit for the Year carried down			

	(Rs)	20__ (Rs)	20__ (Rs)
Sales:			
Less: Bleaching and Processing Charges, Excise Duty, Rebate and Expenses Returns			
Job Contracts			
Closing Stock:			
Finished Goods			
Materials in Process			
Interest:			
On Government and Other Securities			
Less: Income-tax			
Others:			
Less: Income-tax			
Dividend on Shares:			
Less: Income-tax			

Contd...

Exhibit 8 (Contd...)

Profit & Loss Account for the Year Ended March 31, 20__

	Schedule	20__ (Rs)	20__ (Rs)		20__ (Rs)	20__ (Rs)
				Rent from Properties		
				Surplus on Sale of Assets (Net)		
				Miscellaneous Receipts		
					===	===
				Excess Provision in Previous Years		
				Tax Refunds and tax provisions no longer required		
				Balance brought down		
Expenses in respect of Previous Years						
Interim dividend on Equity Shares						
Dividend Equalisation Reserve						
General Reserve						

Exhibit 9

Profit and Loss Account for the Year ended 31st march, 20__

	Schedule No.	20__ Rupees in lakhs	20__ Rupees in lakhs
INCOME			
Sales (less Returns)			
Miscellaneous	13		
EXPENDITURE			
Cost of Materials	14		
Staff Costs	15		
Other Expenses	16		
Interest	17		
Excise Duty			
Depreciation			
(Increase) Decrease in Work-in-Process and Finished Goods	18		
PROFIT BEFORE TAXATION			
Provision for Taxation			
PROFIT AFTER TAXATION			
Add: Balance of Profit brought forward from previous year			
BALANCE APPROPRIATED AS UNDER			
APPROPRIATIONS			
Investment Allowance Reserve			
Proposed Dividend (subject to deduction of tax) @ 15% (20__ 15%)			
GENERAL RESERVE			
NOTES ON ACCOUNTS	19		

individual operative functions as to facilitate their regrouping on the lines advocated.

The profit and loss account reproduced below (figures omitted for the sake of convenience) has been published by the Indian subsidiary

MULTIPRODUCTS LIMITED
Profit and Loss Account for the Year ended March 31, 20__

	Notes	20__ Rs	20__ Rs
SALES AND INCOME			
Sales			
Other Income	1		

Contd...

COSTS AND EXPENSES			
Cost of Sales	2		
Selling, Administrative			
and General Expenses	3	_____	_____
INTEREST			
PROFIT BEFORE TAXATION			
Deduct — Taxation			
Investment			
Allowance Reserve		_____	_____
NET PROFIT FOR THE YEAR			
		=======	========

Exhibit 10

MULTI PRODUCTS LIMITED

Profit & Loss Account for the Year ended March 31, 20__

	Notes	20__ Rs	20__ Rs
INCOME :			
Product Sales	1		
Other Sales	2		
Other Income		_____	_____
		_____	_____
EXPENDITURE :			
Consumption of Materials	3		
Salaries, Wages & Bonus	4		
Interest	5		
Depreciation			
Other Expenses	6		
Provision for Doubtful Debts			
Provision for Gratuity	7		
PROFIT BEFORE TAX			
PROVISION FOR TAX			
PROFIT AFTER TAX		_____	_____
		_____	_____
APPROPRIATIONS :			
Profit after Tax brought down			
Profit on Disposal of Fixed Assets(Net)			
Investment Allowance Reserve not required			
Provisions Relating to Previous years	8		
Balance from Last Year		_____	_____
		_____	_____
Appropriated to :			
Debenture Redemption Reserve			
Investment Allowance Reserve			
General Reserve			
Dividends	9		
Balance carried forward		_____	_____

Exhibit 11

Schedule showing Items of Expenditure Entering the Computation of Cost of Sales and Making-up Selling, Administrative and General Expenses

Items	Cost of Sales	Selling Administrative & General Expenses
Opening Stocks		N.A.
Purchase of Raw Materials		N.A.
Freight		N.A.
Power and Fuel		N.A.
Salaries, Wages and Bonus		
Contribution to Provident and other Funds		
Workmen and Staff Welfare Expenses		
Provision for Termination		
Gratuities and Benefits		
Consumable Stores		N.A.
Repairs & Maintenance to Buildings & Equipment		
Repairs and Maintenance to Machinery		
Rent		N.A.
Insurance		
Rates and Taxes		
Remuneration to Director & Managing Director	N.A.	
Depreciation		
Depletion		
Other Expenses		N.A.
	———	———
Less: Materials used in Construction, etc.		N.A.
Closing Stocks		N.A.
	———	———
	═══	═══

(N.A. : Not Applicable)

of another multinational company. It will be noted that, though being a single step statement like most other profit and loss accounts, it provides separate figures for sales, other non-operative income, cost of sales, selling, administrative and general expenses, and interest paid on borrowings. Depreciation charges are not shown separately because it has been allocated to each individual department. With the help of details supplied in appended notes (not reproduced here), it is easy to recast the published profit and loss account on the lines recommended.

Using the information supplied, the analyst can prepare a statement as in Exhibit 28 showing the profit earned at successive stages of operation and subject the profit and loss account to thorough analysis as explained in Chapter 23 to bring out points of strength and weakness in the operating structure of the company. The terms used in preparing the statement are explained in the paragraphs that follow.

Sales or Revenue

The realisation from the sale of goods or services should be stated gross with deductions for returns allowances, rebates, discounts and commissions, and excise duty shown separately. The resulting figure is net sales.

Most companies show returns, rebates and allowances as straight deductions from gross sales and provide an indication as to whether their products or merchandise are meeting the reasonable requirements of their customers and clients. A high percentage of returns and allowances is always indicative of wide dissatisfaction on the part of the customers.

Discounts or commissions to dealers or selling or agents are frequently included among the expenses items on the ground that they represent payment for services received. In almost all cases, discounts and commissions are trade and quantity discounts, that is, adjustments in selling prices, and are not items of expenditure. They should, therefore, be deducted from gross sales along with returns, rebates and allowances.

The relationship between gross sales and the amount of discounts and commissions represents a measure of the ease with which the company's product or services can be sold. Well-known brands sell quicker while newer or less popular ones require special efforts to secure customer acceptance. A company in a weaker competitive position has to allow a larger discount or commission to its dealers and agents for their extra efforts.

Treatment of excise duty paid differs widely. With rare exceptions, all manufactured products are subject to excise levies at varying rates and in almost all cases such levies are recovered from clients and customers by including them in selling prices of goods sold. Since the amounts of excise duty collected from customers are repayable to the Central Government, they should be deducted from gross sales the same way as are returns, rebates, allowances, discounts and commissions.

Most published accounts show excise duty recovered and paid as an expense item. Some companies, however, show it as a deduction from gross sales while quite a few do not bring the excise duty into the picture at all and report sales net of excise duty paid. The correct procedure from an analytical point of view is to state sales inclusive of excise duty and to show the amount of duty recovered and paid as a deduction along with other deductions such as returns, allowances and discounts. This helps to bring out the relationship between gross sales and the excise duty paid to government and it is particularly useful where the incidence of excise levy on different competing products — cotton, rayon, silk, woollen, nylon and polyester fabrics — is being studied.

In many manufacturing businesses, special attention should be given to the sale of scrap and by-products. If the material sold is scrap, the revenue from its sale should be recorded as a deduction from the cost of manufacture or processing of raw materials. If it is an intermediate product, the revenue earned on its sale should be shown as a separate item in the sales section.

The deduction from gross sales of returns, rebates, allowances, discounts, commissions and excise duty, and the adjustment of sale of scrap and by-products, yields the amount of net sales. This is the effective volume of business on which a profit is earned, or a loss is sustained, and must be shown for the computation of certain ratios essential in determining the operational and financial soundness of the business enterprise under study.

Cost of Goods Sold or Cost of Sales

For mercantile businesses, that is, wholesalers and retailers, this section shows the cost of goods available for sale or sold during the period and equals the opening stock plus purchases less the closing stock. Also included are all expenses connected with the purchasing and storing of goods meant for sale such as freight inward, handling costs, storing and warehousing expenses, insurance charges, returns, allowances and discounts on purchases. Selling, administrative and general expenses are excluded.

In the case of manufacturing enterprises, cost of goods sold comprises cost of raw materials and supplies, direct labour and all manufacturing expenses like power and fuel, repairs and maintenance, rent, rates, taxes, and insurance, and depreciation of factory building, plant, machinery and equipment. The schedule appearing as Exhibit 11 shows the items to be included in computing the cost of goods sold or the cost of sales.

It can be said as a generalisation that companies do not show separately in their published accounts the details of manufacturing costs and it is well-nigh impossible to get the correct figure of the cost of goods sold. There are exceptions, however, and special schedules are appended to the profit and loss account to show details of manufacturing expenses and expenses on selling, administrative and general activities of the business.

Gross Margin

By deducting the cost of goods sold from net sales one arrives at the gross margin on sales. This is frequently referred to as gross profit but the term gross margin is to be preferred because gross profit is generally construed to mean the profit after all expenses but before providing for depreciation and taxation and also prior appropriations.

The most important single figure in the computation of the gross margin and the final net profit is the value of the stock as at the end of the year. If this figure happens to become understated, purposely or accidentally, the profit will have been understated to the extent of the amount by which the closing inventory has been shown less.

Since the closing inventory for one year is the opening inventory for the following year, the profit of that year will be increased by the same amount provided there are no further errors or adjustments. Conversely, when the closing stock figure is overstated, the profit and loss account will show a profit which is higher than the actual by the amount of the overstatement.

Operating Expenses

Expenses incurred in the selling, buying, and general administrative functions of the business are often clubbed together as operating expenses. In a detailed statement, these items are broken down into at least three main divisions — selling, administrative, and general. Selling expenses are those which are incurred directly by the sales department and include salaries of officers, salesmen and other employees of the department, travelling and conveyance expenses of salesmen, advertisement and sales promotion expenses, entertainment expenses and the like.

Administrative and general expenses cover salaries of officers and clerical staff, cost of general administration and supervision, maintenance of accounting, purchase, legal and secretarial record, general correspondence and the such.

There are certain items which are common to all of the three departments. These include rent, rates, taxes and insurance, repairs and maintenance, depreciation of building, furniture and equipment, telephone, telegraph and postage, water and electricity, printing and stationery and so on. These should be allocated to the three departments on some equitable basis.

Operating Profit

Gross profit on deduction of selling, administrative and general expenses yields the operating profit or the operating income for the period. If a provision has been made for doubtful debts, that is, bills which are likely to be incollectible, it should be deducted as an item of expenditure. Also captioned as net operating profit or income, this figure represents the profit or income from normal operations before allowing for income tax and non-operating income and expenses. It provides a measure of the ability of the management to operate the business successfully to the main purpose for which it was established.

Other Income and Expenses

Besides the revenue earned from the sale of goods and services, larger companies earn income by way of rent of property or premises let out, interest and dividend on investment, gains on foreign exchange transactions, commission, and royalty. Such income, though normally small in comparison with the operating income, is closely related to the main functions of the business but since it varies from company to company it should be shown separately for the sake of comparison.

Other expenses include interest on loans, loss on foreign exchange transactions, miscellaneous non-operating expenditure. By having a separate item of interest paid at this stage, the number of times the interest is covered by the operating income or profit, can be easily computed.

This is an important relationship in investment analysis particularly in cases where a large debenture loan is outstanding. Where the item represents interest on short-term loans from banks and others, the comparison is of little relative importance.

Profit Before and After Income Tax

When other income is added to the operating profit and other expenses are deducted, the resulting figure is captioned "Profit before Income Tax". On deducting therefrom the income tax payable on the year's profit, what is left is the "Profit after Income Tax".

Since the liability for income tax for a particular year is only tentative until a final assessment is made by the Income Tax Department, the normal practice is to make a provision for the estimated amount of income tax payable and to show it as a deduction from the profit before income tax to arrive at the net profit after tax. Simultaneously, the estimated amount of income tax payable is recorded on the balance sheet as a liability under the heading "Provisions".

Provision for Taxation

The provision for income tax is computed at the standard rate applicable to corporate assessees on the total income for the year inclusive of any exceptional or extraordinary gains and losses recorded during the year.

These non-operating gains and losses arise from transactions which do not recur regularly and do not arise from the normal operations of the firm. Examples of such extraordinary items are (1) profit or loss on sale of fixed assets, (2) profit or loss on sale of temporary investments or from foreign exchange transactions, (3) extraordinary write-down of sundry debtors, inventories and other current assets, and (4) items relating to prior years.

For the purpose of analysis and, especially, for management benefit, a clear distinction between ordinary and extraordinary items is desirable. Whenever such a distinction is made, all extraordinary items of profit or loss are shown 'net', that is, exclusive of income tax payable or deductible. To be more specific, gains are reported after deducting the additional tax payable and, likewise, losses are reported after deduction of the approximate amount of tax saved.

In other words, the "operating" income tax, meaning the tax payable or normal operating profit, remains unaffected by tax savings or additions arising out of inclusion of non-recurrent items in the taxable income.

Although it is preferable from the point of view of the analyst to have extraordinary gains and losses reported net in the profit and loss account, this is hardly ever the experience and exceptional gains and losses are taken into account while computing the liability to income tax.

Reconciliation

It is obvious that with a standard rate of income tax applicable to corporate assessees, there ought to be a fixed relationship between the profit before deduction of income tax and the provision of income tax shown in published profit and loss accounts. Thus, if the rate of corporate income tax is forty percent, the taxable profit should normally be 2.5 times the provision for income tax.

However, almost all published accounts reveal significant variations in the standard relationship for several reasons. The principal ones among these are:

1. A loss brought forward from the preceding year.
2. The deductions or credits allowed by the Income Tax Act vide sections 80-G to Section 80-O.
3. Provisions or reserves reported in the published profit and loss account for such items of expenditure as retirement gratuity or pension, repairs and maintenance, bad debts not recoverable and written off, and contingencies, may not be allowed, by the assessing officer.
4. Expense items posted directly to the balance sheet instead of to the profit and loss account.
5. The difference, if any, in the provision for depreciation as shown in the published profit and loss account and that shown on the income tax return.

As an essential step in the scrutiny of the profit and loss account and to test the dependability of the published figures, the analyst should attempt a reconciliation between the reported profit before taxation and that worked out by multiplying the provision for income tax by the standard ratio.

If the difference between the figures is small and is due to the special credits allowed by the Income Tax Act, no comment is called for and the reported profit figure should be accepted. If the variation is due to a loss brought forward from the previous year, the provision for income tax made in the published accounts should be recalculated by ignoring the loss brought forward. This is necessary to put the net profit figures of successive years on a comparable basis.

But, should the analyst come across a significant discrepancy which he is unable to explain, he should seek enlightenment from the company's management. It is expected that in most cases an intelligent inquiry on a subject such as this will elicit a satisfactory answer.

PART II

Analysis and Interpretation

CHAPTER 15

Introduction to Analysis

Getting to know the various items of assets and liabilities, as also of income and expenditure, is but the first step towards understanding the balance sheet and the profit and loss account — the financial statements as these are jointly referred to — of a commercial and industrial business undertaking. The second, and more important, step is to know how to analyse the data made available and to draw reliable and logical conclusions from such an analysis.

Part One of this book described the construction, form and contents of the financial statements issued by commercial and industrial companies and explained what each item of assets, liabilities, income, and expenditure stood for. In Part Two will now be discussed the different methods and techniques employed in the reading, that is the analysis and interpretation, of the financial statements of business concerns making use of published annual reports of leading public limited companies but without disclosing the names under which they have been registered and the years to which the financial statements relate.

The Companies Act demands the disclosure of every material feature of operation of each limited liability company and to comply with this requirement of the law companies perforce have to provide an amount of information which can be truly voluminous in the case of large public limited companies. Even though the law permits arrangement of the disclosed information under the most convenient heads, the number of items to be studied and interpreted still remains large. All of these items may not be of equal material significance and it would be a waste of time and effort if an analyst were required to subject each of them to detailed and careful study. It is customary, therefore to, first, analyse or break-down the complex set of facts and figures into smaller and simpler elements and, then, explain or interpret the significance of these simplified statements.

Approach to Analysis

Analysis of financial statements may be attempted both by the management of a business concern and people who do not form part of it. The purpose of "Internal" analysis by the management is to study the effects of policies on the financial position and operating results of the company concerned and to measure the efficiency of individual departments and operations. Such an analysis helps top management to exercise control, measure progress against planned objectives, and to take corrective action whenever needed.

"External" analysis by general creditors and investors is aimed at determining the financial strength of the business for the purpose of granting a loan, extending credit facilities, or assessing the safety or attractiveness of purchasing bonds and shares of the concerned company.

The external analyst who attempts to read, that is, analyse and interpret the balance sheet and the profit and loss account of a business enterprise, must not only have a thorough understanding of these statements but must know also what lies at the back of the money data supplied.

He should know something about the industry in which operates the company whose financial statements he is trying to analyse, the conditions prevailing in that industry, and the changes that are taking place therein. He should also know something about the company itself and should be able to visualise mentally the various departments to the total picture presented by the balance sheet and the profit and loss account.

The analyst should also be aware of the fact that he is dealing with information which is old and that the situation as revealed by the balance sheet might have changed, at times substantially. Similarly, he should be alert to the possibility that he is dealing with incomplete or insufficient financial information. He should go carefully through not only the principal financial statements and the schedules appended thereto, but must also read carefully the notes and clarifications provided and the reports of the directors and the independent auditors to the shareholders, for additional information on specific items. If possible, he should try to get supplementary information and clarification for a more thorough and complete analysis.

Posting the Data

Having collected the required information, the analyst should, as the next logical step, proceed to post it in statement blanks specially prepared for the purpose of analysis in accordance with his views and objectives of study. Although published balance sheets and profit and loss accounts are almost uniform in layout, the forms recommended by the Companies Act or those usually adopted by business corporations, may not necessarily be suitable to meet the requirements of the analyst.

As was pointed out in Part One, the classification of balance sheet items varies considerably and these variations are due to (1) management's intentions and policies, (2) the multiplicity of purposes which the financial statements are to serve, (3) differences in opinions of those who prepare the statements, and (4) difference in the knowledge and experience of the accountants.

It is necessary, therefore, that the analyst recast or reconstruct the financial statements in accordance with his views and purpose of study, and to render them directly comparable. The other objectives which can be achieved by reconstructing the financial statements are (1) to reduce the number of figures by combining similar items and (2) to have available sub-totals in addition to detail amounts for computing ratios, averages and percentages.

Statement Blanks

Most commercial banks and leading institutions have their own printed statement blanks which they require their clients to fill up and submit when putting in an application for a loan. The analyst may adopt one of these forms for the purpose of his analysis, or he may suitably modify it to meet his particular requirements. To assist him in his task, specimen forms prepared according to the principles developed in Part One are presented in Exhibits 12 and 13.

In each instance, columns are provided for tabulating comparative data. More columns may be included depending upon the number of years' data to be analysed. Speaking generally, ten to twelve years' comparative data should prove adequate for any analysis.

In either form, space may be provided for posting additional items as also space to strike sub-totals wherever necessary. Assets are to be posted net, that is, exclusive of provisions, reserves and depreciation. Sales are to be posted gross with deductions for excise duty, returns, allowances, rebates and commission shown separately.

Once the posting is over the analyst may proceed to analyse the data to study relationships and trends and to determine whether or not the financial position, operating results and the general progress of the business are satisfactory.

Methods of Analysis

A number of methods and techniques have been devised to help the analysis and interpretation of the balance sheet and the profit and loss account. These include

1. *Comparative Analysis* showing the changes — in absolute rupee amounts, percentages or ratios — that have taken place in individual items, groups of items or computed items (such as net working capital or tangible net worth) from the balance sheet between two or more balance sheet dates or, in the case of the profit and loss account, during one or more accounting periods.

Exhibit 12

NAME OF COMPANY

Comparative Balance Sheet as at March 31, 20____

Items	20__ Rs	20__ Rs	20__ Rs	20__ Rs	20__ Rs	20__ Rs
ASSETS						
Current Assets:						
Cash						
Marketable Securities						
Acceptances Receivable						
Sundry Debtors – Net						
Inventories						
Prepaid Expenses						
Other Current Assets						
Total Current Assets						
Long-term Investments						
Advances to Subsidiaries & Affiliates						
Miscellaneous Assets						

Items	20__ Rs	20__ Rs	20__ Rs	20__ Rs	20__ Rs	20__ Rs
LIABILITIES & NET WORTH						
Current Liabilities:						
Acceptances Payable						
Sundry Creditors						
Cash Credit & Overdrafts						
Deposits						
Current Amount – Funded Debt						
Provision for – Taxation						
– Dividend						
Other Current Liabilities						
Total Current Liabilities						
Long-term Loans						
Deferred Liabilities						
Total Liabilities						

Contd....

Exhibit 12 (Contd...)

Items	20__ Rs	20__ Rs	20__ Rs
Fixed Assets:			
Land			
Buildings			
Plant, Machinery & Equipment	—	—	—
Less: Depreciation	—	—	—
Add: Capital Work-in-Progress	—	—	—
Fixed Assets – Net			
Intangibles			
TOTAL ASSETS	=====	=====	=====

Items	20__ Rs	20__ Rs	20__ Rs
Net Worth:			
Share Capital: Preference			
Equity			
Total Share Capital	—	—	—
Capital Reserves			
Share Premium Account			
Revenue Reserves	—	—	—
Total Reserves	—	—	—
Total Net Worth	—	—	—
TOTAL LIABILITIES & NET WORTH	=====	=====	=====

Exhibit 13

Name of Company

Comparative Profit & Loss Account for the Year ended March 31, 20___

	20___ Rs	20___ Rs	20___ Rs	20___ Rs
Gross Sales				
Less-				
Returns & Allowances				
Discounts & Commissions				
Excise Duty Paid	___	___	___	___
Net Sales				
Cost of Goods Sold				
Gross Margin on Sales	___	___	___	___
Operating Expenses:				
Selling				
Administrative				
General	___	___	___	___
Operating Income				
Non-Operating Income				
Non-Operating Expenses	___	___	___	___
Total Income				
Interest	___	___	___	___
Profit Before Income Tax				
Provision For Income Tax	___	___	___	___
Profit After Income Tax				
Extraordinary Gains (Net)				
Extraordinary Losses (Net)	___	___	___	___
Profit for Appropriation				
Appropriations:				
Investment Allowance Reserve				
Dividend -Preference				
-Equity				
General Reserve				
	====	====	====	====

2. *Analysis of Trend Relatives,* that is, studying the direction — upwards or downwards — in which individual items, groups of items or computed items from the balance sheet and the profit and loss account have moved over a period of years in relation to their level in a base or standard year.

3. *Common-size Statements* wherein the balance sheet and profit and loss account data are shown as analytical percentages instead of in rupee amounts, the intention being to study the changes that have taken place from year-to-year in individual items in relation to the total of assets, total of liabilities, and total net sales.

4. *Statement of Changes in Net Working Capital* studying the increase or decrease in net working capital during the interval between two balance sheet dates and listing the specific sources from which working capital has been obtained and the various uses or applications of the working capital.
5. *Statement of Sources and Application of Funds* demonstrating the amount of funds that has flown into the business in the interval between two balance sheet dates and from which sources, and also how these funds have been used or applied.
6. *Cash-flow Statement* revealing the movement of cash into and out of the business.
7. *Standard Ratios* measuring the relationships between two items, or groups of items, which are both in the balance sheet or in the profit and loss account, and between items from the profit and loss account on the one hand and items from the balance sheet on the other.

Types of Analysis

Analysis of the balance sheet or the profit and loss account using the above methods and techniques can either be internal or external. Internal analysis is concerned with the study of the relationship between items, groups of items or computed items from the balance sheet, or the profit and loss account, or both, for the same year with the help of standard ratios or common-size percentages.

External analysis involves the comparison with the help of percentages or ratios, of the same items, groups of items or computed items in two or more balance sheets of the same business enterprise on different dates, and the profit and loss account for different years.

To be comprehensive, analysis of the balance sheet and the profit and loss account must be both internal as well as external. Comparative or external analysis of the financial status of business not assisted by internal ratio analysis can often be misleading.

Terms like "horizontal or dynamic" and "vertical or static" are sometimes used to describe the analytical measures — ratios and percentages employed. When the financial statements of a business concern for a number of successive years are analysed, the term "horizontal or dynamic" is applied since the analysis tends to bring to light the year-to-year trend or movement in individual items in the balance sheet and the profit and loss account.

The other expression, "vertical or static", is employed to refer to the method of studying the financial statement for a single year. An analysis of this nature merely reveals the relationship between individual items from the balance sheet and the profit and loss account, or between individual items and the total of assets, the total of liabilities, and total net sales. All ratio analysis is essentially static.

CHAPTER 16

Interpretation of Comparative Statements

A balance sheet exhibits the assets and liabilities of a business enterprise as at a particular date. It also provides, for the sake of comparison, the values and amounts of assets and liabilities as they appeared in the books of the company exactly one year earlier. The profit and loss account, likewise, shows items of income and expenditure as well as the final profit or loss for the year just ended and for the one preceding it.

An average individual, however, is unable to grasp the significance of the changes that may have taken place over the year in individual items unless the rupee amounts for the two years are posted side-by-side in vertical comparative columns and the changes that have taken place are worked out either in absolute rupee amounts or in ratios or percentages.

The method of studying the relationship between items, groups of items (such as current assets or current liabilities), or computed items (like net worth or net working capital) from the balance sheet and the profit and loss account of the same business enterprise for two or more years is known as comparative statement analysis.

Its purpose is to analyse the financial statements of a commercial and industrial business concern with the view of computing the changes that have taken place between two balance sheet dates or from year to year, in individual items of assets and liabilities and, further, to studying whether such changes have been favourable or unfavourable.

Exhibit 14 presents in a summarised form the comparative balance sheet of Engineering Products Ltd. as at March 31, 2001 and 2002, the intervening year having seen some significant changes in the company's structural and financial positions. The first two columns in the table carry the actual balance sheet data for the two years. Column 3 gives the increases or decreases during 2002 in rupee amounts while Column 4 shows the percentage increase or decrease in individual items between the two balance sheet dates.

The advantage of showing the changes that have taken place during the year in absolute rupee amounts is that, major changes become evident and point the way to further study, investigation, and interpretation. Small or minor changes can be ignored and need not be taken up for further consideration.

Studying only the absolute rupee data has the drawback, however, that it does not bring to light proportionate changes that have taken place between the balance sheet dates. For example, absolute amounts may show sundry debtors and sundry creditors both having increased by Rs 10,00,000 but may not bring out the fact that while sundry debtors have increased by 20 percent, sundry creditors have gone up by 50 percent.

To bring out relative changes in individual balance sheet items it is more useful to show, in addition to absolute amounts, the increases or decreases in percentages. Such percentages are obtained by dividing the increases or decrease in each item by the amount of that item on the earlier year's balance sheet and multiplying the resulting figure by 100%.

If, for instance, sundry debtors as at March 31, 2002 were more by Rs 81,00,000 than as at March 31, 2001, the increase in sundry debtors between the two balance sheet dates was seven per cent as follows:

$$\frac{\text{Rs } 81,00,000}{\text{Rs } 11,54,00,000} \times 100 = 7.0\%$$

The foregoing method of analysis can also be used to compare the profit and loss accounts of a business for two or more years and to investigate whether the results of its operations and its financial progress have been satisfactory or unsatisfactory. Exhibit 15 shows in a summarised form, the comparative profit and loss accounts of Engineering Products Ltd. for the years ended March 31, 2001 and 2002.

If monthly or quarterly profit and loss accounts are being prepared, comparison may be made with the corresponding month or quarter of the preceding year or years. Cumulative totals for the elapsed period may be computed and averages can be worked out and analysed.

When the profit and loss account for successive years is being studied, it is often advantageous to work out the annual averages for the period of study as a whole in addition to the increases or decreases that have taken place in individual years. The idea is to study how each year's figures compare with the average for the period under scrutiny.

Since the average tends to level out the ups and downs of the business, it becomes possible, by employing the method of comparative analysis, to spotlight the favourable and unfavourable tendencies that might have developed during individual years and to discover the factors responsible for them. Exhibit 16 illustrates this point.

Instead of showing increases or decreases in absolute rupee amounts or percentages, it is sometimes convenient to express them in terms of ratios because this obviates the need to use minus or negative signs wherever decreases have taken place. A ratio of less than one means that there has been a decrease while a ratio in excess of one indicates

Exhibit 14

ENGINEERING PRODUCTS LIMITED
Comparative Balance Sheet as at March 31, 2001 and 2002

Items	March 31 2001	March 31 2002	Increases or Decreases During 2002	
	Rs Lakhs	Rs Lakhs	Rs Lakhs	%
ASSETS				
Current Assets				
Cash	46	86	40	87.0
Sundry Debtors	1154	1235	81	7.0
Inventories	684	718	34	5.0
Other Current Assets	130	119	-11	-8.5
Total Current Assets	2014	2158	144	7.2
Long-term Investments	127	157	30	23.6
Fixed Assets – Net	773	866	93	12.0
Miscellaneous Assets	74	147	73	98.7
TOTAL ASSETS	2988	3328	340	11.4

Contd...

Exhibit 14 (Contd...)

ENGINEERING PRODUCTS LIMITED

Comparative Balance Sheet as at March 31, 2001 and 2002

Items	March 31		Increases or Decreases During 2002	
	2001	2002		
	Rs Lakhs	Rs Lakhs	Rs Lakhs	%
LIABILITIES AND NET WORTH				
Current Liabilities	1879	1804	-75	-4.0
Long-term Loans	327	449	122	37.3
Total Liabilities	2206	2253	47	2.1
Net Worth				
Share Capital- Preference	15	111	96	640.0
Equity	401	452	51	12.7
Reserves - Capital	26	63	37	142.3
Revenue	340	449	109	32.1
Total Net Worth	782	1075	293	37.5
TOTAL LIABILITIES AND NET WORTH	2988	3328	340	11.4

Exhibit 15

ENGINEERING PRODUCTS LIMITED

Comparative Profit and Loss Account for the Years Ended March 31, 2001 and 2002

	Year Ended March 31		Increases or Decreases During 2002	
	2001	2002		
	Rs Lakhs	Rs Lakhs	Rs Lakhs	%
Sales and Services	2772	2962	190	6.9
Less : Materials, Manufacturing and Operating Expenses	1675	1757	82	4.9
Staff Expenses	565	607	42	7.4
Sales and Administrative Expenses	278	283	5	1.8
Depreciation	57	58	1	1.8
Total Cost and Expenses	2575	2705	130	5.0
Operating Income	197	257	60	30.5
Non-operating Income — Net	106	126	20	18.9
Total Income	303	383	80	26.4
Interest and Brokerage	108	110	2	1.9

Contd...

Exhibit 15 (Contd...)

ENGINEERING PRODUCTS LIMITED

Comparative Profit and Loss Account for the Years Ended March 31, 2001 and 2002

	Year Ended March 31 2001	Year Ended March 31 2002	Increases or Decreases During 2002	
	Rs Lakhs	Rs Lakhs	Rs Lakhs	%
Profit before Tax	195	273	78	40.0
Provision for Tax	69	102	33	47.8
Profit after Tax	126	171	45	35.7
Tax Adjustment for Previous Years	—	5	5	
Transferred to Reserves	126	176	50	39.7

an increase in the items between the two balance sheet dates. This is made clear by the following table

| | As at March 31 | | Increases or Decreases | | |
	20__ Rs Lakhs	20__ Rs Lakhs	Amount Rs Lakhs	Percentage (%)	Ratio
Cash	17	12	-05	-29.4	0.71
Sundry Debtors	74	98	+24	+32.4	1.32
Prepaids	6	2	-04	-66.7	0.33
Inventories	160	163	+03	+1.9	1.02
Current Liabilities	395	471	+76	+19.2	1.19
Current Assets	257	275	+18	+7.0	1.07

The method can be employed to analyse and study the balance sheets for a series of years. When this is attempted, comparisons may be made either with the data of the earliest year of the series as shown in Part I of Exhibit 17 or with the data of the immediately preceding year as shown in Part II of the Exhibit.

Comparative Analysis — Interpretation

Engineering Products Limited

When the comparative balance sheet and the profit and loss account have been prepared and changes, either in actual rupees or in percentages, have been computed, the analyst should proceed to study those items showing only significant changes. He should consider them individually — or jointly where they are directly related — to determine, if possible, the reasons for the variations and whether or not the changes are favourable.

For instance, if net sales have risen by a certain percentage it may be due to a larger quantity of goods sold, or an increase in the selling price, or both. Similarly, if there has been an increase in the amount of sundry debtors, it may have been due to (1) a larger volume of sales, (2) a change in the credit terms granted to customers, (3) inability of some clients to meet their liability on time, or (4) the inability of the company itself to collect its receivables promptly.

The comparative balance sheet of Engineering Products Ltd. as at March 31, 2001 and 2002 (Exhibit 14) indicates that during 2001-2002 the net worth of the company increased by Rs 293 lakh or, 37.5 percent, and that this was due to (1) an increase of Rs 96 lakh in the preference share capital, (2) an increase of Rs 51 lakh in the equity share capital, and (3) an increase of Rs 146 lakh in reserves of which Rs 37 lakh were of a capital nature and Rs 109 lakh of a revenue nature.

Exhibit 16

STAMP-FORGE INDIA LIMITED

Comparative Profit and Loss Accounts for Year ended March 31, 20___

(Amounts — Rupees in Lakhs)

Items	Year A	Year B	Year C	Total	Average
Net Sales	5,467	4,883	5,561	15,911	5,304
Cost of Sales *Less* Depreciation	4,384	3,904	4,518	12,806	4,269
Gross Profit	1,083	979	1,043	3,105	1,035
Depreciation	207	214	231	652	217
Selling, Administrative and General Expenses	477	345	338	1,160	387
Operating Income	399	420	474	1,293	431
Non-Operating Income	310	245	258	813	271
Total Income	709	665	732	2,106	702
Interest Paid	388	420	346	1,154	385
Profit before Taxation	321	245	386	952	317
Provision for Taxation	70	20	138	228	76
Profit after Taxation	251	225	248	724	741
Investment Allowance Reserve	120	88	44	252	84
Balance for Appropriation	131	137	204	472	157

Exhibit 17

PART I

| | Year Ended March 31 | | | Increases or Decreases | | | |
	Year A Rs Lakhs	Year B Rs Lakhs	Year C Rs Lakhs	Year B over Year A Rs Lakhs	%	Year C over Year A Rs Lakhs	%
Net Sales	1804	2342	2565	538	29.8	761	42.2
Profit before Tax	357	409	498	52	14.6	141	39.5
Net Working Capital	433	562	618	129	29.8	185	42.7
Net Worth	658	773	763	115	17.5	105	16.0
Fixed Assets – Net	259	249	250	-10	-3.9	-9	-3.5

PART II

| | Year Ended March 31 | | | Increases or Decreases | | | |
	Year A Rs Lakhs	Year B Rs Lakhs	Year C Rs Lakhs	Year B over Year A Rs Lakhs	%	Year C over Year B Rs Lakhs	%
Net Sales	1804	2342	2565	538	29.8	223	9.5
Profit before Tax	357	409	498	52	14.6	89	21.8
Net Working Capital	433	562	618	129	29.8	56	10.0
Net Worth	658	773	763	115	17.5	-10	-1.3
Fixed Assets – Net	259	249	250	-10	-3.9	1	-0.4

During the year two important structural changes took place in the company. Approval of the High Court and other appropriate authorities was received for the amalgamation with the company of one of the subsidiaries, namely, William Butler India Ltd. in which Engineering Products held 93 per cent interest. The amalgamation became effective from April 1, 2000, and 13,249 equity shares of Rs 10 each were issued during the year to the outside shareholders in exchange for their holding in the merged company.

The second development was the merger with Engineering Products Ltd. of the Capstan Bank Ltd. whose banking business was nationalised in July 1999. The shareholders of the Bank were allotted 1,91,610 preference shares of Rs 50 each; 5,10,960 equity shares of Rs 10 each; and 8% convertible bonds and 8 % redeemable bonds of the combined face value of Rs 1,24,55,000.

The rise of Rs 37 lakh in the capital reserve represented the surplus from the net assets of the bank taken over under the terms of the merger. The increase of Rs 109 lakh in the revenue reserves represented the profits retained in the business as shown by the following table:

ENGINEERING PRODUCTS LIMITED

**Statement of Retained Profits for the Years ended March 31,
2001 and 2002**

	Year Ended March 31	
	2001	2002
	Rupees in Lakhs	
Opening Balance	264	340
Add : Profit for the year Transferred from the Profit and Loss Account	127	171
	391	511
Less : Dividends for the Year on Preference and Equity Shares	51	65
	340	446
Add : Transferred from Provision for Income Tax for prior year	—	5
	340	451
Less : Doubtful Advances written off	—	2
Closing Balance	340	449
	===	
Less Opening Balance		340
Net Increase in Revenue Reserves during 1972		109
		===

Other important changes which took place during the year were:

1. Long-term loans increased by Rs 122 lakh, or 37.3 per cent, because of the issue of bonds of the aggregate value of Rs 125 lakh to shareholders of the merged bank. Other long-term loans decreased by Rs 2,48,000 on payment of the annual instalments.

2. The increase in net worth and long-term loans was accompanied by a decrease of Rs 43 lakh in sundry creditors and of Rs 91 lakh in short-term loans. But, because of the combined increase of Rs 59 lakh in the provisions for taxation and dividends, the net decrease in current liabilities was Rs 75 lakh including minor changes in other dues and obligations.

3. As compared with the four per cent decrease in current liabilities, current assets increased by 7.2 per cent, or Rs 144 lakh. This improved the company's working capital position with net working capital increasing by Rs 219 lakh, or 162 per cent, from Rs 135 lakh to Rs 354 lakh.

4. Sundry debtors, including bills of exchange held, increased by seven per cent and inventories went up five per cent. As compared with these changes, net sales advance 6.9 per cent. A larger sales volume was, thus, accomplished with a relatively smaller inventory and relatively unchanged amount of sundry debtors as at March 31, 2002 giving a more favourable turnover of inventories during 2001-2002.

Although, this reflects a favourable tendency, the analyst should ask a number of questions before coming to any definite conclusion. In particular, he should inquire:

a. Whether the relatively lower level of inventories as at March 31, 2002 was typical of the monthly averages for the year or there was any "window-dressing" involved to present a better financial picture as at the year-end.

b. Was the slower rate of rise in inventories compared with sales due to (1) intentional sales before the end of the year, (2) reduced costs, (3) inability to replace the stocks consumed, (4) change in the policy with respect to the level of inventories to be maintained, or (5) a change in the method of valuation of inventories.

c. Did sales increase rapidly because of (1) greater efficiency of the sales department (2) improvement in trading conditions, (3) a widening of the product range, or (4) special year-end sales.

5. Long-term investments increased by Rs 30 lakh or 23.6 per cent, because of fresh investments in some of the associated companies and the purchase during the year of 2,98,000 equity shares (Rs 5 paid-up) of Star Petro-Chemical Industries Corporation Ltd. from whom, possibly, important construction contracts were secured.

6. Fixed assets, gross, increased by 11.6 per cent during the year but the net block was higher at the year-end by 12 per cent because of the larger capital work-in-progress. The rate of increase in net fixed assets was much faster, however, than the rate of increase in net sales which was 6.9 per cent.

It must be noted that the profitability or otherwise of plant expansion cannot be judged from the results of the year of the expansion. This is because there may be teething troubles to overcome, the assets are usually operative only for a part of the year, and some time must elapse before markets can be located for the expanded production. In the case of Engineering Products Ltd., the increase in net fixed assets during 2001-2002, may be reflected in net sales of future years.

7. As mentioned, income by way of sales and services rose by 6.9 per cent from Rs 2,772 lakh to Rs 2,962 lakh, but expenses increased by only five per cent from Rs 2,575 lakh to Rs 2,705 lakh. In other words, income from sales and services, and operating expenses did not increase percentagewise in the same proportion. As a result, operating income rose from Rs 197 lakh to Rs 257 lakh, or 30.5 per cent.

With the non-operating income also significantly higher and interest charges only a shade larger, the profit before taxation was up 40 per cent to Rs 273 lakh from Rs 195 lakh in the preceding year and although this necessitated a much enlarged provision of Rs 102 lakh as against Rs 69 lakh, for taxation, the profit after tax was still 35.7 per cent higher at Rs 171 lakh as compared with Rs 126 lakh for 2000-2001.

8.   Even at the enhanced level the provision for taxation was only 37.4 per cent of the profit before taxation as compared with the then standard rate of 55 per cent. Additional detailed information is required to explain this variation.

The analyst must always remember that the provision for income tax is computed on the basis of ordinary regular income as well as extraordinary income and, further, there is always a difference between the accounting income as shown on the published profit and loss account and the income reported in the income tax return because of the several factors mentioned in Chapter 15.

CHAPTER 17

Interpretation of Trend Relatives

The method of analysis described in the foregoing chapter is useful in studying the changes which may have taken place from one year to another, or from some "standard" year, in individual items of assets, liabilities and net worth. If it is desired to determine and study the direction — upward or downward — in which the items have moved in successive years in relation to their levels at the start of the period of study or at any suitable date, trend analysis may be employed.

In this method of analysis, items from the balance sheet and the profit and loss account of a business for a number of successive years are posted in parallel vertical columns in such a way that the same item from each balance sheet, or each profit and loss account, appears on the same horizontal line, and then the percentage relation which individual items bear to their "base year" levels is computed to reveal the direction in which the business and its financial characteristics have developed.

These trend percentages, or trend relatives as they are often called, reveal the proportionate changes that have taken place in individual items since the base year and enable the analyst to form an opinion, by comparing the trend data, whether the financial position of the business is improving or deteriorating.

The base year may be the earliest year of the period under study or any intermediate year. Generally, the first year of the period is taken as the base year unless abnormal trading conditions are known to have prevailed during that year and the amounts of that year are not typical of those which follow it.

To get the trend relative or index number, each item in the balance sheet or the profit and loss account of the base year is taken as 100 per cent and the same item in each of the statements to be compared is expressed as a percentage of the base year figure.

For instance, if closing inventories were Rs 460 lakh in year A, the base year, and Rs 546 lakh in Year F, the trend relative would work out to 118.7 per cent as follows:

$$\frac{\text{Closing Inventories (Year F) Rs 546 lakh}}{\text{Closing Inventories (Year A) Rs 460 lakh}} \times 100 = 118.7\%$$

This may be rounded off to 119 per cent. Other percentages can be calculated in the same manner and fractions may be ignored or rounded off to the nearest integer because balance sheet items do not reflect exact measurements.

It is to be noted that trend percentages do not reveal the actual increases or decreases that might have taken place in an item since the base year. To obtain a measure of such increases or decreases it is necessary to deduct 100 from the trend percentage.

In the foregoing illustration, closing inventories for Year F were 119 per cent of those for Year A which is the same thing as to say that closing inventories for Year F were 19 per cent higher than for Year A.

Instead of computing trend percentages for the balance sheet and the profit and loss account items, trend ratios may be computed to furnish the same information. This is done quite simply by dividing the trend percentages by 100. A ratio of less than 1.00 will indicate a decrease and one in excess of 1.00 will indicate an increase. The following summary data make this clear:

	Year A	Year F
Current Assets		
Amount (Rs 000)	8,250	9,990
Trend Percentage	100	121
Trend Ratio	1.00	1.21
Current Liabilities		
Amount (Rs 000)	7,020	6,720
Trend Percentage	100	96
Trend Ratio	1.00	0.96
Net Sales		
Amount (Rs 00)	14,430	20,520
Trend Percentage	100	142
Trend Ratio	1.00	1.42

Although trend percentages can, and often are, computed for each item in the balance sheet or the profit and loss account, only those items are generally taken for study or analysis which have some logical relationship with one another.

For instance, if sales have doubled over a period of, say, five years, it will be instructive to see what has been the percentage or relative increase in such balance sheet items as operating assets, inventories, and sundry debtors. Likewise, the trend in current assets should be compared with the trend in current liabilities.

What this means is that one trend alone is not fully informative and various related trends should be compared and interpreted. Such a comparison of related trends proves highly valuable to the analyst particularly if his analysis extends over a period of years.

In order to explain this method of analysis, the rupee and trend data of the Indo British Corporation Ltd. for the six-year period ended

March 31, Year A through Year F both inclusive, are presented in Exhibits 18 and 19.

Trend Percentages — Interpretation

Indo British Corporation Limited

Indo British Corporation is the oldest and largest manufacturer of a range of products vitally needed by the indigenous engineering industry. It has established manufacturing units at several important locations throughout the country so as to be able to cater to the requirements of its clients more effectively. Its comparative balance sheet in Exhibit 18 reveals the following favourable and unfavourable trends in its financial position.

1. There was no significant change in the "current" financial position of the company as revealed by a comparison of current assets with current liabilities. The former increased from Rs 714 lakh as at March 31, Year A, to Rs 1,059 lakh as at March 31, Year F, that is, by 48 per cent in five years, while the latter increased in the same period from Rs 490 lakh to Rs 739 lakh or 51 per cent. Because of the somewhat larger percentage increase in current liabilities, net working capital expanded by only 43 per cent from Rs 224 lakh to Rs 320 lakh.

Moreover, because of the almost parallel increase in current assets and current liabilities, the current ratio measuring the relationship between the two, remained more or less stationary at 1.4 times though it was a shade higher at 1.6 times during the three years D-F, inclusive. For the entire period of six years, however, the ratio was well below the accepted standard of rupees two of current assets for every rupee of current liabilities.

The data further reveal that inventories increased during the six-year period from Rs 356 lakh to Rs 548 lakh, that is, by 54 per cent; sundry debtors from Rs 262 to lakh Rs 354 lakh, or 35 per cent; and 'quick' assets (comprising cash, sundry debtors, and loans and advances) from Rs 358 lakh to Rs 511 lakh, or 43 per cent.

The faster rate of growth of inventories was fully justified by the 58 per cent increase in net sales from Rs 1,496 lakh to Rs 2,367 lakh. The relatively smaller amount of sundry debtors reflect a more rapid turnover of customer accounts and a more favourable collection experience.

1. Fixed assets, net, decreased during the period under review by 28 per cent from Rs 847 lakh to Rs 613 lakh. As mentioned earlier, net sales increased during the same period by 58 per cent. On the face of it, this indicates a more intensive use of plant facilities since a larger turnover was realised on relatively smaller total net fixed assets.

But, the larger increase in net sales might have been due to an increase in selling prices, a greater sales promotional programme, more efficient and effective salesmanship, or a larger volume of goods sold. The trend of the physical volume of sales should be studied before drawing firm conclusions.

The decrease in net fixed assets does not mean that there was no addition at all to fixed assets or no acquisition from the beginning of the period till its end. In fact, the book value of buildings, plant, machinery and equipment (not shown in the table) increased by 16 per cent while gross fixed assets, including capital work-in-progress, were some 11 per cent higher as at March 31, Year F than five years previously.

But since March 31, Year A, accumulated depreciation increased by 59 per cent, or Rs 404 lakh, from Rs 683 lakh. This brought down the value of the depreciated block by Rs 234 lakh to Rs 613 lakh as at March 31, of Year F.

The factor responsible for the relatively slower rate of increase in the value of gross fixed assets as compared with the rate of increase of accumulated depreciation was that in more recent years there was a perceptible slow-down of the tempo of capital spending and during the five years, A through F, Indo British Corporation Ltd. spent only Rs 170 lakh on acquiring new assets as against Rs 120 lakh in year A and Rs 280 lakh in the preceding year.

Five years previous to the start of the period under review, the Corporation had drawn up a programme of substantial development and expansion to be completed during the next four years and requiring an outlay of Rs 600 lakh. The programme was completed as scheduled and the five years up to the end of Year F were spent in consolidating the gains from the expansion.

There was, therefore, relatively smaller capital expenditure during these years but the depreciation charge on the expended block remained high. It is interesting to note that the cost of the expansion was fully recovered by way of the annual depreciation charged to the profit and loss account during the next ten years.

2. Current liabilities as at March 31, Year F, were larger by Rs 249 lakh, or 51 per cent than those as at March 31, Year A. Deferred liabilities, representing provision for retirement gratuity payable to employees for past services, increased by Rs 30 lakh or 176 per cent, while term-loans decreased by Rs 222 lakh or 76 per cent consequent upon repayment of mid-term loans from banks and an unsecured loan from the parent company in Great Britain.

A break-down of current liabilities would show that, between March 31, Year A and March 31, Year F, sundry creditors, including

Exhibit 18

INDO BRITISH CORPORATION LIMITED
Comparative Balance Sheet as at March 31, 20___

Items	Amounts – Rupees in Lakhs						Trend Percentages (Year A = 100%)					
	Year A	Year B	Year C	Year D	Year E	Year F	Year B	Year C	Year D	Year E	Year F
ASSETS											
Current Assets :											
Cash	34	42	53	37	40	63	124	156	109	118	188
Sundry Debtors	262	299	293	284	323	354	114	112	108	123	135
Inventories	356	314	337	393	419	548	88	95	110	118	154
Other Current Assets	62	52	55	54	90	94	84	89	87	145	152
Total Current Assets	714	707	738	768	872	1059	99	103	108	122	148
Miscellaneous Assets	130	126	118	122	131	154	97	91	94	101	118
Fixed Assets – at cost	1530	1557	1585	1613	1659	1700	102	104	105	108	111
Less: Depreciation	683	776	868	946	1021	1087	114	127	139	149	159
Fixed Assets – Net	847	781	717	667	638	613	92	84	79	75	72
TOTAL ASSETS	1691	1614	1573	1557	1641	1826	95	93	92	97	108

Contd....

Exhibit 18 (Contd...)

INDO BRITISH CORPORATION LIMITED
Comparative Balance Sheet as at March 31, 20___

Items	Amounts – Rupees in Lakhs						Trend Percentages (Year A = 100%)					
	Year A	Year B	Year C	Year D	Year E	Year F	Year B	Year C	Year D	Year E	Year F	
LIABILITIES & NET WORTH												
Current Liabilities	490	440	458	477	596	739	90	94	97	122	151	
Deferred Liabilities	17	23	27	34	49	47	135	159	200	288	276	
Long term Loans	294	264	201	119	76	72	90	68	40	26	24	
Total Liabilities	801	727	686	630	721	858	91	86	79	90	107	
Net Worth :												
Equity Share Capital	462	462	462	462	462	462	100	100	100	100	100	
Reserves	428	425	425	465	458	506	99	99	109	107	118	
Total Net Worth	890	887	887	927	920	968	100	100	104	103	109	
TOTAL LIABILITIES AND NET WORTH	1691	1614	1573	1557	1641	1826	95	93	92	97	108	

Exhibit 19

INDO BRITISH CORPORATION LIMITED

Comparative Profit and Loss Accounts for Year A-F, Ended March 31, 20___

(Amounts — Rupees in Lakhs)

Items	Year A	Year B	Year C	Year D	Year E	Year F
Net Sales	1496	1450	1586	1737	2052	2367
Cost of Goods Sold	1146	1130	1233	1334	1626	1887
Gross Margin	350	320	353	403	426	480
Selling, Administrative and General Expenses	176	173	191	205	219	254
Operating Income	174	147	162	198	207	226
Non-operating Income less Expenses	8	9	13	13	12	10
Total Income	182	156	175	211	219	236
Interest	32	31	23	21	17	19
Profit before Tax	150	125	152	190	202	217
Provision for Tax	70	67	92	78	129	149
Profit after Tax	80	58	60	112	73	68

Contd...

Exhibit 19 (Contd...)

INDO BRITISH CORPORATION LIMITED

Trend Percentages

Year A = 100 per cent

Items	Year B	Year C	Year D	Year E	Year F
Net Sales	97	106	116	137	158
Cost of Goods Sold*	99	108	116	142	165
Gross Margin	92	101	115	122	137
Selling, Administrative and General Expenses*	98	109	116	124	144
Operating Income	85	93	114	119	130
Non-operating Income less Expenses	113	165	165	150	125
Total Income	86	96	116	120	130
Interest	97	72	66	53	60
Profit before Tax	83	101	127	135	145
Provision for Tax	96	132	112	184	213
Profit after Tax	73	75	140	91	85

* Depreciation and common items of expenditure have not been allocated.

trade acceptances, advanced by 87 per cent from Rs 228 lakh to Rs 426 lakh; provisions for taxation and dividends by 77 per cent, or Rs 98 lakh, to Rs 225 lakh; while short-term loans decreased by Rs 48 lakh, or 36 per cent, to Rs 86 lakh. Thus, the company appeared to be depending more on its trade creditors than on its bankers for a part of its working capital requirements.

The 87 per cent increase in trade creditors as compared with 58 per cent in net sales clearly shows that the company experienced a shortage of working capital, a fact corroborated by the lower-than-average current ratio.

3.   A comparison of the trends in total liabilities and in net worth reveals that while the former increased during the last five years by seven per cent, the rate of growth of the latter was a shade faster at nine per cent and that, as at March 31, Year F, net worth formed 52.9 per cent of total of liabilities and net worth as compared with 52.7 per cent as at the start of the period under review.

In other words, there was no significant strengthening of the financial position of the company which still depended to a large extent on creditor funds for its short-term and long-term requirements. The principal factors responsible for the slow rate of increase of net worth were (1) no additional share capital was issued during any one of the five years, (2) a low average rate of return on invested capital, and (3) the distribution of a high percentage of the available net profit as dividend on equity shares. It is to be noted, however, that in spite of the high pay-out ratio, the rate of dividend was no better than 12 per cent during the first three years, 14 per cent for the next two, and 15 per cent for Year F.

4. It will be observed from the rupee and trend data for net sales, costs and profits (Exhibit 19) that the increase in cost of goods sold had always been out of proportion to the increase in net sales and, for that reason, gross margin on sales had been always depressed. Between Year A and Year F, sales increased by 58 per cent or Rs 871 lakh from Rs 1,496 lakh to Rs 2,367 lakh, but cost of sales advanced from Rs 1,146 lakh to Rs 1,887 lakh, that is, by 65 per cent.

As said, this restricted the growth of gross margin which improved by only 37 per cent from Rs 350 lakh to Rs 480 lakh. Selling, administrative, and general expenses also rose faster than gross margin with the result that operating income could register a rise of only 30 per cent in five years.

The company was, thus, unfortunate in not having been able to fully counterbalance rising costs of manufacture and other expenses by increasing the output and sale of products. Its efforts to maximise the utilisation of its productive facilities and extend its turnover were hampered, in particular, by the political uncertainty and labour unrest in the State where some of its major units are located, general industrial recession, slow rate of pick-up of industrial activity, and shortage of certain basic raw materials.

The data also indicate that the only favourable trend was the 40 per cent decrease in interest charges which followed as a consequence of the repayment of long-term loans and was mainly responsible for the somewhat faster increase of 45 per cent in the profit before tax. But, this was more than offset by the 113 per cent increase in the provision for taxation and, as a result, the profit after tax showed a decrease of 15 per cent at Rs 68 lakh.

CHAPTER 18

Common-size Statements

A business concern obtains funds from diverse sources which may be broadly classified as (1) the owners who contribute the permanent share capital, (2) profits earned from operations and retained in the form of reserves, (3) providers of short-term and long-term loans such as banks, financial institutions and the public, and (4) sundry creditors for goods supplied or services rendered. The funds procured from these different sources appear as liabilities on the firm's balance sheet and are invested in various types of assets classified as current and non-current.

During the course of analysis and interpretation of balance sheets, it is often found necessary to investigate whether the relative importance of different sources and applications of funds has undergone significant shifts, and to search for the factors that may have been responsible for them. The purpose of such an analysis and interpretation is to find out if the firm is tending to place a growing reliance on a particular source of funds or is investing excessively in particular assets, current or non-current.

The methods discussed in the preceding two chapters do not, speaking generally, enable the analyst to comprehend and visualise, except casually, the changes in individual items of liabilities and assets that are taking place because there exists no common basis for comparison when dealing with the absolute rupee amounts supplied by the annual financial statements.

Common-size Balance Sheet

Such a common basis for comparison becomes available, however, if the balance sheet and profit and loss account items are expressed as analytical percentages of the balance sheet total that is, by showing each item of liabilities as a percentage of the total of liabilities and net worth and, similarly, each asset as a percentage of total assets. When so shown, the balance sheet and the profit and loss account are designated common-size statements.

Such statements prove useful in (1) analysing the current financial position and operating results of individual companies, (2) comparing the financial standing and operating performance of one company with that of another in the same line of business or with that of the industry as a whole, and (3) to a lesser extent, making a historical study of the changes that may have taken place over the years in the financial position or operating performance of individual companies.

To prepare common-size statements from the usual "rupee" statements simply:

1. state total assets, total liabilities and net worth, and net sales as 100 per cent,
2. compute the percentage ratio of each balance sheet item to the statement total, and each computed item from the profit and loss account as a percentage of net sales.

If, for instance, total assets of a business as at the balance sheet date are worth Rs 4,957 lakh and closing inventories are worth Rs 1,857 lakh, then inventories are 37.5 per cent of total assets as follows:

$$\frac{\text{Closing Inventories}}{\text{Total Assets}} = \frac{\text{Rs 1,857 lakh}}{\text{Rs 4,957 lakh}} = 37.5\%$$

Percentages for other items of assets can be computed in the same manner. As for individual items of liabilities, each item will be computed as a percentage of the total of liabilities and net worth.

It will be appreciated that the common-size percentage method represents a type of ratio analysis because each individual item of the balance sheet, or the profit and loss account, is expressed as a percentage of the statement total. It must be noted, however, that since the percentages represent component parts of the totals, a horizontal comparison from year to year would result only in a study of the relationship.

In other words, unlike in trend analysis, the growth or decline in the financial position of the business cannot be detected from the common-size percentages and only changes in the data relative to the total for a particular date or period can at best be determined.

If the rate of increase in an item is slower than the rate of increase of the total, the item, expressed in rupees, will show a decreasing percentage of the total. If the rate of decrease of the total is faster than the rate of decrease in an item, the item will show an increasing percentage of the total.

The value of common-size statement is considerably enhanced if an additional column is provided for each year to show the percentage of each item in a group to the total of the group. For example, each item of current assets can be expressed as a percentage of total current assets as well as of total assets. Exhibit 20 demonstrates the method.

Exhibit 20

TITAN ENGINEERING LIMITED
Balance Sheet as at March 31, 20__

	Rupees in Lakhs	Percent of Sub-total	Percent of Total
ASSETS			
Current Assets-			
Cash	201	0.55	0.29
Sundry Debtors	14,955	41.17	21.66
Inventories	18,759	51.64	27.18
Other Current Assets	2,412	6.64	3.49
Total Current Assets	36,327	100.00	52.62
Non-Current Assets	6,720		9.73
Fixed Assets-Net	25,993		37.65
TOTAL ASSETS	69,040		100.00
	=====		=====
LIABILITIES			
Current Liabilities-			
Sundry Creditors	12,315	36.38	17.84
Other Current Liabilities	21,535	63.62	31.19
Total Current Liabilities	33,850	100.00	49.03
Deferred Liabilities	14,560		21.09
Total Liabilities	48,410		70.12
Net Worth			
Preference Share Capital	134	0.65	0.19
Equity Share Capital	5,308	25.73	7.69
Reserves	15,188	73.62	22.00
Total Net Worth	20,630	100.00	29.88
TOTAL LIABILITIES & NET WORTH	69,040		100.00

Common-size Profit and Loss Account

Common-size percentages for balance sheet items are undoubtedly useful since they reveal the relationship between individual items and the totals. This relationship gets somewhat distorted, however, if total assets include "non-operating" assets such as long-term investments, deferred expenses or assets which are not used in connection with regular operations of the business.

This is particularly true when two or more companies having different amounts of these assets are being compared, or, when in the balance sheet of the same company, these items have increased or decreased violently over the years.

More useful, especially to the management, are common-size percentages for items in the profit and loss account because of the obvious relationship which exists between net sales and the cost of goods sold, gross margin, operating expenses, operating profit and net profit or loss.

Common-size profit and loss account is more frequently used, therefore, and is prepared from the "rupee" statement in exactly the same manner as is prepared the common-size balance sheet from the rupee balance sheet.

Net sales are expressed as one hundred per cent and the various expenses items are expressed as percentages of net sales. The profit and loss account of Powerpack India Ltd. for the year ended March 31, 20___, below explains the method.

POWERPACK INDIA LIMITED
Profit and Loss Account for the Year ended March 31, 20___

	Amount Rs Lakhs	Per cent %
Net Sales	6,245	100.00
Cost of Goods Sold	4,485	71.82
Gross Margin	1,760	28.18
Selling, Administration and General Expenses	377	6.04
Operating Income	1,383	22.14
Non-operating Income	95	1.52
Total Income	1,478	23.66
Interest	94	1.50
Profit before Tax	1,384	22.16
Provision for Tax	824	13.19
Profit after Tax	560	8.97

Common-size Percentages — Interpretation

Paragon Tyres India Limited

The common-size balance sheets as at March 31, Year A — Year F, of Paragon Tyres India Ltd. (Exhibit 21) shows that significant rupee and percentage changes took place in several of the items, especially, between March 31, Year C and March 31, Year F. An increasing number of paise of each asset rupee was invested in land, buildings, plant, machinery, and other non-current assets than in current assets. In

Exhibit 21

PARAGON TYRES INDIA LIMITED
Comparative Balance Sheet as at March 31, 20___

Items	Amounts – Rupees in Lakhs						Common-size Percentages					
	Year A	Year B	Year C	Year D	Year E	Year F	Year A	Year B	Year C	Year D	Year E	Year F
ASSETS												
Current Assets :												
Cash	29	21	18	111	234	103	0.9	0.6	0.5	2.6	4.4	2.1
Marketable Securities	11	16	17	18	16	18	0.4	0.5	0.4	0.4	0.3	0.4
Sundry Debtors	870	854	1007	877	1011	622	27.8	24.7	25.3	20.4	19.2	12.5
Inventories	1036	1309	1462	1612	1713	1857	33.2	37.8	36.7	37.6	32.6	37.5
Other Current Assets	207	176	242	214	250	260	6.6	5.1	6.1	5.0	4.8	5.2
Total Current Assets	2153	2376	2746	2832	3224	2860	68.9	68.7	69.0	66.0	61.3	57.7
Miscellaneous Assets	105	115	130	173	226	284	3.4	3.2	3.3	4.0	4.3	5.7
Fixed Assets – at cost	1765	1965	2203	2511	3100	3284	56.5	56.8	55.3	58.5	59.0	66.3
Less: Depreciation	899	995	1100	1222	1292	1471	28.8	28.8	27.6	28.5	24.6	29.7
Fixed Assets – Net	866	970	1103	1289	1810	1813	27.7	28.0	27.7	30.0	34.4	36.6
TOTAL ASSETS	3124	3461	3979	4294	5260	4957	100.0	100.0	100.0	100.0	100.0	100.0

Contd...

Exhibit 21 (Contd...)

Items	Amounts – Rupees in Lakhs						Common-size Percentages					
	Year A	Year B	Year C	Year D	Year E	Year F	Year A	Year B	Year C	Year D	Year E	Year F
LIABILITIES & NET WORTH												
Current Liabilities												
Sundry Creditors	460	526	676	773	1333	1225	14.7	15.2	17.0	18.0	25.3	24.7
Short-term Loans	169	276	508	484	513	171	5.4	8.0	12.8	11.3	9.8	3.5
Other Current Liabilities	334	405	265	288	411	496	10.7	11.7	6.6	6.7	7.8	10.0
Total Current Liabilities	963	1207	1449	1545	2257	1892	30.8	34.9	36.4	36.0	42.9	38.2
Long-term Loans	458	455	518	538	550	447	14.7	13.1	13.0	12.5	10.5	9.0
TOTAL LIABILITIES	1421	1662	1967	2083	2807	2339	45.5	48.0	49.4	48.5	53.4	47.2
Net Worth :												
Share Capital												
- Preference	70	70	70	70	70	70	2.2	2.0	1.8	1.6	1.3	1.4
- Equity	1000	1000	1000	1000	1000	1000	32.0	28.9	25.1	23.3	19.0	22.2
Reserves	633	729	942	1141	1383	1448	20.3	21.1	23.7	26.6	26.3	29.3
TOTAL NET WORTH	1703	1799	2012	2211	2453	2618	54.5	52.0	50.6	51.5	46.6	52.8
TOTAL LIABILITIES AND NET WORTH	3124	3461	3979	4294	5260	4957	100.0	100.0	100.0	100.0	100.0	100.0

other words, there was a realignment or redistribution of the asset rupee, non-current assets claiming a larger portion than current assets.

The data also reveal that outside finance or creditor funds constituted a relatively more important source of the capital invested in assets than shareholders' funds or net worth particularly up to March, 31, Year E. Thus, creditors provided 53.4 per cent of the total funds invested is assets as at March, 31, Year E, as against 45.5 per cent as at the end of Year A.

The share of funds provided by the owners themselves declined steadily during the same period from 54.5 per cent of the total invested funds to 46.6 per cent. There was a welcome improvement in the concluding year of the six-year period when a rights issue of equity shares was made at a premium of Rs 11 for a share of Rs 10. As a result, owners' contribution to invested funds increased to 52.8 per cent and that of the creditors naturally declined to 47.2 per cent as at the end of Year E.

The period covered by the study was one of substantial expansion of Paragon Tyres' productive facilities at its two factories. In Year B the company commenced work aimed at enlarging the capacity of its plant at Calcutta in a significant way and while the work was still in progress, Paragon Tyres set about to enhance the capacities of its other factory for making automotive tyres, tubes and bicycle rims. Both of these projects were completed by the end of Year E.

With the view to meeting the foreign exchange component of the finance needed, the company negotiated a long-term loan with its parent company abroad. The Rupee Finance was, as planned originally, to be raised from internal cash generation. But since additional finance of about Rs 200 lakh was also needed, a rights issue of 10 lakh equity shares of Rs 10 each was made at a premium of Rs 11 a share towards the close of Year F.

The following table shows the distribution of major items of assets and liabilities as at March 31 of Year A and of Year F.

	Year A		Year F	
	Rs Lakhs	%	Rs Lakhs	%
Current Assets	2,153	68.9	2,860	57.7
Fixed Assets Net	866	27.7	1,813	36.6
Other Non-Current Assets	105	3.4	284	5.7
Total Assets	3,124	100.00	4,957	100.00
Current Liabilities	963	30.8	1,892	38.2
Long-term Loans	458	14.7	447	9.0
Net worth	1,703	54.5	2,618	52.8
Total-Liabilities and Net Worth	3,124	100.00	4,957	100.00

As a result of successive expansions, the gross block increased by Rs 1,519 lakh in five years (Exhibit 21) and represented 66.3 per cent of total gross assets as at March 31, Year F as compared with 56.5 per cent five years earlier. Although the amount of accumulated depreciation rose by Rs 572 lakh, net assets were still larger by Rs 947 lakh and claimed 36.6 per cent of each asset rupee in contrast to 27.7 paise as at the end of Year A.

The net worth increased during the five years by Rs 915 lakh to Rs 2,681 lakh inclusive of the additional funds brought in by the rights equity issue. But, even then, it represented only 52.8 per cent of the total funds invested in the business as at March 31, Year F.

The significant fact to note is that the entire amount of cash-flow (increase in net worth plus increase in accumulated depreciation) of Rs 1,487 lakh generated during the period was used up in acquiring fixed assets and there was nothing available either to repay, even partly, long-term loans or to strengthen the current financial position which had shown some deterioration owing to over-rapid expansion.

While the expansion of the factories was being carried out, there was a steady buoyancy of the markets and a rising demand for the company's widening range of products. Net sales increased between Year A and Year F by 46 per cent from Rs 5,128 lakh to Rs 7,490 lakh even though full advantage of the completion of the expansion could not be availed of owing to labour trouble at one of the factories in Year F.

The increase in sales necessitated the maintenance of larger inventories which increased in value by 80 per cent from Rs 1,036 lakh to Rs 1,857 lakh and absorbed 37.5 paise of every asset rupee as at March 31, Year F as compared with 33.2 paise as at the end of Year A. Sundry debtors increased between Year A and Year F in absolute rupee amounts, but not percentagewise and, in fact, claimed a successively decreasing portion of total assets.

As at March 31, Year A, sundry debtors claimed 27.8 paise of each asset rupee but five years later the proportion declined to just 12.5 paise in a rupee. The decline in the relative importance of sundry debtors was due to a stricter control on credit expansion and the introduction of an improved bill collection procedure.

Since, as mentioned earlier, internal resources were found inadequate to provide the working capital needed to support a growing volume of sales, Paragon Tyres India Ltd., had to rely increasingly for its short-term financial requirements on creditor funds. From Year A through Year F, there was a rapid increase in both sundry creditors and short-term borrowings from banks and others. The former went up from Rs 460 lakh to Rs 1,333 lakh and the latter from Rs 169 lakh to Rs 513 lakh.

With these increases the contribution of current creditors to total capital funds increased to 42.9 per cent as at March 31, Year E from

Exhibit 22

PARAGON TYRES INDIA LIMITED

Comparative Profit and Loss Account for Years A-F, Ended March 31, 20___

(Amounts – Rupees in lakhs)

Items	Year A	Year B	Year C	Year D	Year E	Year F
Net Sales	5128	5550	6430	6897	7619	7490
Cost of Goods Sold	4161	4467	5193	5622	6329	6486
Gross Margin	967	1083	1237	1275	1290	1004
Selling, Administrative and General Expenses	407	463	511	544	625	673
Operating Income	560	620	726	731	665	331
Non-operating Income less Expenses	9	29	42	70	58	59
Total Income	569	649	768	801	723	390
Interest	53	48	69	97	120	139
Profit before Tax	516	601	699	704	603	251
Provision for Tax	260	328	283	302	225	75
Profit after Tax	256	273	416	402	378	179

Contd....

Exhibit 22 (Contd....)

PARAGON TYRES INDIA LIMITED
Common-size Percentages (Net Sales = 100 per cent)

Items	Year A	Year B	Year C	Year D	Year E	Year F
Net Sales	100.0	100.0	100.0	100.0	100.0	100.0
Cost of Goods Sold	81.2	80.5	80.8	81.5	83.1	86.6
Gross Margin	18.8	19.5	19.2	18.5	16.9	13.4
Selling, Administrative and General Expenses	7.9	8.3	7.9	7.9	8.2	9.0
Operating Income	10.9	11.2	11.3	10.6	8.7	4.4
Non-operating Income	0.2	0.5	0.6	1.0	0.8	0.8
Total Income	11.1	11.7	11.9	11.6	9.5	5.2
Interest	1.0	0.9	1.0	1.4	1.6	1.9
Profit before Tax	10.1	10.8	10.9	10.2	7.9	3.3
Provision for Tax	5.1	5.9	4.4	4.4	2.9	0.9
Profit after Tax	5.0	4.9	6.5	5.8	5.0	2.4

30.8 per cent four years earlier. Long-term loans remained almost unchanged but represented a relatively less important source of capital funds. The issue of equity shares in the Year F raised the owners' contribution to 52.8 per cent from 46.6 per cent a year ago, but short-term creditors still constituted an important source of the company's working capital needs.

The common-size profit and loss account of the company (Exhibit 22) shows that cost of goods sold, absorbed an increasing percentage of net sales during the last three years but had remained relatively steady during the first half of the six-year period. Selling, administrative, and general expenses as well as interest charges also absorbed increasingly more of the sales rupee and the profit before estimated income-tax, therefore, decreased both in absolute rupee amounts and percentagewise.

This was due principally to rising raw material prices, substantial increases in personnel costs, larger provisions for depreciation, power shortage, and labour troubles. The increases in cost due to these diverse factors completely neutralised the benefits which accrued owing to the upward revision in prices of tyres and tubes made effective from the middle of Year C.

Common-size Percentages — Interpretation

Comparison of Two Companies

The common-size balance sheet and profit and loss account of two comparable companies can be studied to detect differences and to bring out, if possible, the percentages that are most likely to be desirable from the point of view of effective financial and operating efficiency. Exhibit 23 presents the common-size balance sheet as at March 31, of Company A and Company B, which manufacture almost identical products and are otherwise generally comparable. The following differences in the financial position of the two companies may be noted.

1. Company A appears to be in a weaker financial position compared with Company B because it has, in relation to total liabilities and net worth, share capital and reserves of only 23.5 per cent whereas Company B has 41.7 per cent. Both the companies, however, have made a larger use of creditor funds than of funds provided by the owners.

2. The current financial position of Company A is also decidedly weaker than that of Company B. Current liabilities of the former company represent 70 per cent of the total funds employed in the business while current assets have absorbed only 63 per cent of these funds. Company A, therefore, has a negative amount of net working capital and a current ratio of less than 1.00.

Exhibit 23

Company A and Company B
Common-size Balance Sheet as at March 31, 20__

	Company A		Company B	
	Amount Rs Lakhs	Per cent of Total	Amount Rs Lakhs	Per cent of Total
ASSETS				
Current Assets :				
Cash	106	8.9	68	7.6
Sundry Debtors	170	14.2	80	8.9
Inventories	450	37.7	465	52.0
Other Current Assets	26	2.2	4	0.5
Total Current Assets	752	63.0	617	69.0
Miscellaneous Assets	9	0.8	12	1.4
Fixed Assets – Net	432	36.2	265	29.6
Total Assets	1,193	100.0	894	100.0
LIABILITIES & NET WORTH				
Current Liabilities	837	70.1	355	39.7
Long-term Loans	76	6.4	166	18.6
Total Liabilities	913	76.5	521	58.3
Net Worth :				
Share Capital — Preference	45	3.8	—	—
Equity	107	9.0	157	17.5
Reserves	128	10.7	216	24.2
	280	23.5	373	41.7
TOTAL LIABILITIES & NET WORTH	1,193	100.0	894	100.0

In the case of Company B, current liabilities have contributed only 39.7 per cent of total liabilities and net worth, whereas current assets claim 69 per cent of the total funds invested. The current ratio of Company B, therefore, exceeds 1.00 and the current creditors enjoy a wider margin of safety.

3. Company A has 14.2 per cent of its total assets in the form of sundry debtors whereas Company B has 8.9 per cent. This means that Company B has a better collection procedure and a stricter control on credits. Again, Company B has larger inventories than Company A but this is justified by the former company's larger sales volume.

4. Company A has invested more in net fixed assets than has Company B. This may mean that Company A has a larger plant or that Company B has depreciated its gross block faster than has Company A. The larger the cost of net or depreciated fixed assets in relation to the net sales value the less favourable the operating results are likely to be.

5. The common-size profit and loss account of the two companies given below shows that the cost of goods sold by Company B amounts to 79.8 per cent of net sales whereas the same item for Company A is 88.2 per cent. Consequently, Company B has been able to secure a higher percentage of gross margin and a larger profit before tax than has been Company A.

Company A and Company B
Common-size Profit & Loss Account for the Year ended March 31, 20___

| | Company A | | Company B | |
	Rs Lakhs	%	Rs Lakhs	%
Net Sales	1,218	100.0	1,528	100.0
Cost of Sales	1,074	88.2	1,219	79.8
Gross Margin	144	11.8	309	20.2
Operating Expenses	101	8.3	77	5.0
Operating Income	43	3.5	232	15.2
Non-operating Income	6	0.5	—	—
Profit before Tax	49	4.0	232	15.2
Provision for Tax	10	0.8	151	9.9
Profit after Tax	39	3.2	81	5.3

CHAPTER 19

Analysis of Working Capital

The working capital of a business reveals the strength or weakness of its current financial condition. The financial state of a business is constantly changing, however, and the changes taking place with the passage of time have important implications for the owners and the management of the business as well as for the short-term creditors who have money at stake in the business in the form of trade credit or short-term loans.

The changes by themselves have little significance unless they provide answers to two pertinent questions. First, what is the present composition of current assets or the gross working capital and, second, if changes have taken place therein, what have been the reasons for these changes and whether the changes are favourable or unfavourable.

For example, the working capital of a firm may have increased from Rs 1,524 lakh to Rs 2,449 lakh and the change may appear favourable. But, no firm conclusion can be drawn without studying the composition of the gross working capital, that is, total current assets employed in the business. The increase of Rs 925 lakh, or 61 per cent, may have been due to an excessive rise in the book-value of sundry debtors or an over-investment in stocks of raw materials or of finished goods. The former may prove slow of recovery and the latter slow of consumption or turnover. In either situation, the working capital would become less liquid than previously. The increase in working capital, then, cannot be pronounced as favourable.

In a reverse situation, working capital might have decreased by Rs 925 lakh, but the reason thereof might have been a more efficient collection of outstanding bills leading to a decrease in book debts, or a faster liquidation of inventories. If such has been the case, the change, though indicating a decrease, will have to be considered favourable.

Again, an increase in working capital may have been the result of one or more of such financial transactions as (1) issuance of additional shares for cash, (2) issuance of debenture bonds, (3) sale of non-current assets, or (4) increase in operating profit.

An increase in working capital resulting from a larger plough-back of current profit would have to be interpreted differently from an increase brought about by the issuance of shares or bonds. Likewise, a decrease in working capital should not be viewed as unfavourable if analysis reveals a strengthening of the current financial position in spite of it. Again, a change in working capital following a reduction in current liabilities should be adjudged more favourable than one resulting from an increase in non-current assets.

In other words, no final judgement on the change in working capital can be passed without (1) studying the distribution of the different current assets within the totality of such assets to assess the relative importance of the constituent assets, (2) working out, in absolute rupee amounts as well as in percentages, the changes that may have taken place over a period to look for shifts in management policies, and (3) investigating the causes for the increases and decreases in working capital items.

The first two steps require the application of methods already described in the preceding two chapters and will be elaborated upon in the following pages. The third step requires discussion of the technique used in preparing a statement listing the sources and application of working capital and will be explained in a later chapter.

Distribution of Current Assets

It frequently happens that a company seemingly possesses adequate working capital and yet is unable to meet its maturing liabilities in time. Such a situation arises primarily because of an improper distribution of working capital funds among the different current assets.

The cash in hand or in bank, may be well in excess of the normal day-to-day requirements or there may be over-investment either in stocks of raw materials and finished goods or in sundry debtors. Such lapses in policy can be located by studying the distribution of current assets with the help of common-size percentages.

When sales are increasing, a company naturally finds it necessary to carry an adequately large inventory of raw materials and finished goods for the purpose of manufacture and delivery respectively. Hence, it will continue to have a sound current financial position so long as sales and inventories both increase in more-or-less the same proportion.

It happens quite often, however, that the stock-in-trade is allowed to grow faster than net sales in anticipation of future demand. If the anticipated demand does not materialise the company finds itself carrying a far larger stock of raw materials and finished goods than can be turned quickly through the process of sale into cash that can be used to meet the maturing claims of short-term creditors. There, thus, will be an excessive investment in inventories than can be good for the continued financial soundness of the business.

A similar situation would arise if book debts were to be permitted to accumulate either by allowing customers over-liberal credit terms or by failing to collect outstanding bills when due. If book debts are not collected in time, the business would inevitably find itself short of cash to defray day-to-day expenses, to purchase all of the stock-in-trade that would be required, to meet promptly suppliers' bills and other maturing liabilities, and may have to resort to short-term borrowing.

To detect such situations as they tend to emerge, it becomes necessary to study the distribution of the current assets and the relationship individual items bear to the total. This is done by expressing each current asset item as a percentage of the total of all current assets as is done in preparing common-size statements. Again, because a single year's figures cannot be fully informative since they present a static picture, three or more years' data have to be considered to detect favourable and unfavourable changes in individual current assets relative to their total.

A high percentage of inventories in total current assets is usually considered unfavourable because it reveals a less liquid current position. The situation is to be viewed, however, in the light of the circumstances prevailing in particular industries or affecting individual companies.

The working capital in its gross amount is supposed to be more liquid if a proportionately larger amount is invested in cash, marketable securities and sundry debtors than in inventories. This is a generalisation, again, and must not be accepted without further investigation.

In some cases, sundry debtors may be relatively less liquid because some of the bills may not be collectible and no provision might have been made to write them off. The inventories, on the other hand, may be more liquid and can normally be sold at a profit to increase the amount of working capital.

The table below presents distribution of current assets of Indian Metal Corporation Ltd. as at March 31, Year A — Year F, inclusive, in absolute rupee amounts and as common-size percentages. The company operates within the electric arc furnace industry and is a large producer of alloy steel ingots and rolled products for the engineering industry besides aluminium rolled products and sections.

INDIAN METAL CORPORATION LIMITED
Current Assets as at March 31, Year A — Year F

Amounts – Rs Lakhs

As at March 31	Cash	Sundry Debtors	Inventories	Others	Total
Year A	15	403	678	61	1157
Year B	144	447	739	41	1371
Year C	104	312	1113	101	1630
Year D	92	460	988	52	1592
Year E	68	395	1333	82	1878
Year F	114	563	1281	113	2071

Contd../-

	Common-size Percentages			
Year A	1.3	34.8	58.6	5.3	100.0
Year B	10.5	32.6	53.9	3.0	100.0
Year C	6.4	19.1	68.3	6.2	100.0
Year D	5.8	28.9	62.0	3.3	100.0
Year E	3.6	21.0	71.0	4.4	100.0
Year F	5.5	27.2	61.9	5.4	100.0

The absolute rupee data of Indian Metal Corporation shows that while the amount of book debts outstanding as at the end of each year except the concluding one showed only minor fluctuations, the book-value of inventories, mainly finished goods, generally maintained a steady downward trend. The decrease in inventories witnessed during Year D and Year F, was caused by the decline in production owing to shortage of electrical power and the need to liquidate stocks to meet consumer demand which continued to be strong.

The common-size percentages indicate that over the years importance of inventories relative to total current assets increased and that of cash and sundry debtors (the "quick" assets) taken together declined. This indicates that, in its composition, the working capital tended to become less liquid with the passage of time. However, no firm judgement can be passed on the rising trend in the investment in inventories without taking note of the trends in net sales, current assets and current liabilities.

Trend Analysis of Current Assets and Current Liabilities

Common-size percentage of current assets help the analyst to draw preliminary conclusions about the extent of liquidity of the working capital of the firm whose balance sheet is being studied. To get a confirmation of the conclusions drawn, analysis of the changes that may have taken place in individual items of current assets as also of current liabilities, should be undertaken as shown in Exhibit 24.

It needs to be emphasised that by themselves trend percentages indicate nothing more than the direction in which individual items of current assets and current liabilities have moved during the period of study. In interpreting these changes as indicated by trend percentages, it is necessary to study the changes in related items as well.

For example, a declining trend in sundry debtors, or an increasing trend in inventories, must be compared with the trend in net sales. A declining trend in sundry debtors, though indicating that the working capital position is becoming less liquid, is to be considered favourable in the association of a rising trend in net sales because it may indicate effective customer credit and bill collection policies. But, if net sales also display a declining trend, the conclusion could only be that a

Exhibit 24

INDIA METAL CORPORATION LIMITED
Current Assets and Current Liabilities as at March 31, 20__

Items	Amounts – Rs Lakhs						Trend Percentages – Year A = 100%				
	Year A	Year B	Year C	Year D	Year E	Year F	Year B	Year C	Year D	Year E	Year F
CURRENT ASSETS											
Cash and Equivalent	15	144	104	92	68	114	960	694	614	453	760
Sundry Debtors	403	447	312	460	395	563	111	77	114	98	140
Inventories	678	739	1113	988	1333	1281	109	164	146	197	189
Other Current Assets	61	41	101	52	82	113	67	168	85	135	185
Total Current Assets	1157	1371	1630	1592	1878	2071	119	141	138	162	179
CURRENT LIABILITIES											
Sundry Creditors	193	320	467	450	576	412	166	242	233	298	213
Short-term Loans	20	116	11	127	269	647	580	55	635	1345	3235
Provisions	351	305	241	261	327	486	87	69	74	93	138
Accrued Interest	15	20	43	55	54	65	133	287	367	360	433
Other Current Liabilities	66	41	72	68	107	100	62	109	103	162	152
Total Current Liabilities	645	802	834	961	1333	1710	124	129	149	207	265
Net Working Capital	512	569	796	631	545	361	111	155	123	107	71
Net Sales	2158	2109	2642	3540	3994	4410	98	122	164	185	204
Quick Assets	418	591	416	552	463	677	141	91	132	111	162

general deterioration in operations has set in. Similarly an inventory increasing in value year after year and accompanied by stable or declining net sales, would indicate, speaking generally, an increasing investment of working capital funds in inventories and an inefficient marketing policy.

A study of Exhibit 24 reveals that while current liabilities and net sales both showed rising tendencies, current liabilities increased at a much faster rate than both net sales and current assets. The company, in other words, tended to depend more heavily on creditor funds for its working capital needs which exhibited a natural tendency to expand in sympathy with the growing volume of sales. Because of the sharper increase in current liabilities as compared with current assets, net working capital exhibited a declining tendency, climbing down by 29 per cent from Rs 512 lakh to Rs 361 lakh.

Among current assets, sundry debtors advanced by 40 per cent whereas net sales expanded by 104 per cent over five years. This favourable trend indicates that a stricter control was being exercised on credit expansion and that an efficient bill collection procedure was being consistently followed. The 89 per cent increase in inventories was perhaps justified by the 104 per cent expansion in net sales. But, by themselves, inventories formed a larger percentage of total current assets and this rendered the working capital position less liquid.

The increase of Rs 1,065 lakh, or 165 per cent in total current liabilities was due mainly to an increase of Rs 219 lakh in trade creditors and a sharper rise of Rs 627 lakh in current loans inclusive of annual instalment payable against long-term loans. These trends are unfavourable and indicate a growing reliance on creditor funds for build-up of inventories to feed a growing volume of sales. As a result net working capital showed a declining trend after Year C having decreased from Rs 796 lakh to Rs 361 lakh, or 30 per cent below the starting level of Rs 512 lakh.

CHAPTER 20

Introduction to Ratio Analysis

A balance sheet and a profit and loss account present a historical record of the financial position and the results of operations of industrial and commercial business enterprises. The historical data for two or more years can be analysed to determine whether the financial progress of the enterprises had been satisfactory or not and to bring out the general direction in which their finances had moved over the period of study. That is done by employing the techniques of comparative analysis of the balance sheet and the profit and loss account, and trend percentages as explained in Chapters 16 and 17.

An analysis of this nature is mainly described as "external analysis" because it is concerned only with the changes that have taken place in individual items of the balance sheet and the profit and loss account for two or more years. It does not, as a rule, permit the study of the relationship between the different items of the balance sheet and the profit and loss account. Such an "internal" analysis of the relationship of items of the two financial statements is essential for the interpretation of the financial and operating data and for the confirmation of the conclusions drawn from comparative analysis of the financial statements or from the study of trend percentages or ratios.

Standard Ratios

The relationship between items, or group of items, appearing on the financial statements can be expressed mathematically in the form of proportions, ratios, rates or percentages. Thus, if the current assets of a company as at a particular date are Rs 7,00,000 and the current liabilities are Rs 3,50,000, the relationship between current assets and current liabilities can be expressed variously as (1) current assets are two times current liabilities, (2) there are Rs 2 of current assets for every rupee of current liabilities, or (3) current assets are 200 per cent of current liabilities.

The necessity of expressing the relationship between related items in the form of ratios or percentages arises from the fact that absolute rupee data are incapable of revealing the soundness or otherwise of a company's financial position or performance. Net sales of Rs 400 lakh a year may appear satisfactory, but no positive conclusions can be drawn unless they are compared with the book-value of tangible net worth or operating assets.

Again, a single ratio in itself is meaningless because it does not provide a complete picture of a company's financial position. In this respect, a company may be likened to a human body. To be pronounced in perfectly good health, a person must have weight proportionate to his height and age, a certain body temperature, a certain blood-pressure, a certain number of heart beats per minute, and so on. It is only when all or most of these measurements or vital statistics are found to be satisfactory that the person is declared to be physically fit.

The same is true of a company. A single ratio may direct attention to only one aspect of its financial status or operating performance. Unless the other aspects of its financial position are analysed and found to be satisfactory, the company cannot be pronounced to be in good health financially. It is to get as complete a picture as possible of the financial health of a company that a number of ratios are to be computed and studied together.

These ratios can be conveniently classified as:

1. *Balance Sheet Ratios* which deal with the relationship between two items or groups of items which are both in the balance sheet. For example, the ratio of current assets to current liabilities, or the ratio of total liabilities to tangible net worth.

2. *Profit and Loss Account Ratios* which deal with the relationship between two items or groups of items in the profit and loss account. For example, the ratio of cost of goods sold to net sales.

3. *Balance Sheet and Profit and Loss Account Ratios* which deal with the relationship between items from the profit and loss account on the one hand and items from the balance sheet on the other. For example, the ratio of net sales to net working capital, or the ratio of net profit to tangible net worth.

It must he emphasised that, like any other statistical measurement, ratios are only a convenient means of expressing the relationship between two items. They are not final in any sense of the word and cannot be a substitute for "thinking" on the part of the analyst. They are merely a starting point and focus attention on specific relationships which may require further study.

Just as a single ratio may prove inadequate to provide a complete picture, too many ratios may tend to obscure it and confuse the analyst. Only the relationship between important items and groups of items should be computed and interpreted. While trying to interpret the results of his analysis the analyst should bear in mind that a ratio may be "unfavourable" at the extremes of a satisfactory range.

At one end, the ratio may represent a weak and dangerous position, at the other end it may indicate a strong but unprofitable position. A company, for instance, must always have adequate cash to defray its day-to-day expenses. Shortage of cash may force it to default payments and reveal a weak financial position. But excess of cash is equally unfavourable since it means a less profitable use of costly capital.

Measures of Comparison

Rations and percentages have little significance unless they can be compared with, or matched against, appropriate standards. Unless there are available measuring devices or standards, the analyst will not be able to determine whether the ratios indicate favourable or unfavourable conditions. Standards of comparison are of four common types: (1) absolute, (2) historical, (3) horizontal, and (4) budgeted.

Absolute standards are rules of the thumb based on personal experience or observation and are a general conception of what is adequate or normal. They are accepted regardless of the type of business, the time, or the objective of the analyst. The most common example of absolute standards is the rule that current assets should preferably be two times current liabilities or more.

Historical standards are based on the record of the past financial and operating performance of individual business concerns. Ratios or percentages based on past performance of a company cannot serve as reliable standards, however, because of the changes that may have taken place in the character and operations of the company.

All dynamic enterprises are constantly expanding their operations, widening their range of products and diversifying or branching-out into new fields. The conditions prevailing now may be vastly different from those which obtained, say, ten years ago. Besides, accounting policies, procedures, and practices also may have undergone changes which may render historical ratios and percentages unreliable or unsound as standards.

Horizontal or external standards represent ratios and percentages of selected competing companies, especially the most progressive and successful ones, or of the industry of which the individual company is a member. Standard ratios based on the financial and operating data of selected companies or the industry, cannot be thought of as "ideal", however, or even as representing "satisfactory conditions". At best, they are "representative" of the industry and indicate to the individual company what its ratios should be in order to be comparable to the averages of the industry.

Budgeted standards, or "goal ratios" as they are sometimes called, are developed by using the data included in the company's current budget. Such ratios are based on past experience modified by anticipated changes during the account period. Actual ratios are compared with the planned or goal ratios to examine the degree of accomplishment of the anticipated targets.

Since the targets are set on the basis of certain assumptions, they cannot serve as a good measure of results if the assumptions have been basically incorrect or are not realised. If carefully developed, budgeted standards are very useful in financial analysis but external analysts experience difficulties in employing them and must, therefore, rely on historical or horizontal standards.

Industry Standards

The preparation of standard ratios for a group of companies presupposes that all the companies included in the summary are homogeneous, that is, own and operate similar properties and business and perform almost identical functions or stages of manufacture. In actual practice that is hardly ever the case.

Individual companies operating within the same industry vary significantly from each other in size, age, location of their plants, the sources of raw materials, the size and location of markets for finished goods, quality of management, product-mix and product-range, capitalisation, and accounting policies and methods. These later often produce large variations in financial and operating data and in the ratios derived from them.

Again, certain members of an industry may be highly successful and most efficient. Other members may have an unsatisfactory financial condition and operating performance. If ratios of such companies are included in the industry average, there may be a marked up or down shift in the standard which, in that case, may not be typical or representative of the industry. In developing industry standards, therefore, extreme cases should either be excluded or should be given a lower weightage in the computation.

It should be evident from the foregoing that, there being wide variations in the size, location and age of companies, their financial and other policies and accounting conventions, (1) averages of their ratios cannot be precise factual measures or standards in a strict sense, and (2) there is need for one to proceed cautiously in reaching conclusions when the ratios of a single company are being compared with the averages for the industry. Such industry averages only indicate what the ratios of a member of that industry should approximate to if the company is to be representative of the industry. They should be considered by the analyst as starting points for further investigation and analysis.

Average ratios can either be arithmetic averages or median or middle number of individual ratios for a group of companies engaged in the same line of business. For example, if the average ratio of current assets to current liabilities of, say, 20 companies is required, the arithmetic average is obtained by adding up individual ratios and dividing the total by 20. Alternatively, current assets and current liabilities of the 20 companies may be separately totalled up and the ratio of the totals may be computed to give an average ratio.

To find out the median or middle value, the individual current ratios are listed in an ascending or descending order and the middle value is found by inspection. The median is often more representative of a group of ratios than the arithmetic average which, as stated, may reflect extreme items.

CHAPTER 21

Analysis of Current Financial Condition

The owners, managers, and creditors of a business must always keep under scrutiny the firm's current financial condition as revealed by its net working capital. Adequacy of working capital enables the company to carry on its operations comfortably and without financial stringency, to expand its business without the need of new financing, to meet its maturing obligations in time, and to bear occasional losses without having to face a financial disaster.

Shortage of working capital produces the opposite results. It causes delays in settling creditors' claims and loss of credit-standing, and prevents the company from taking advantage of opportunities for expanding its business operations. In more severe cases, it leads to insolvency and a winding-up.

The improvement or deterioration in net working capital is brought to light by trend relatives, common-size percentages and statements showing the changes that have taken place between two balance sheet dates separated by one or more years. The conclusions drawn from such an "external" analysis, however, need to be supported by an "internal" analysis involving a study of the relationship between individual items of current assets, current liabilities, and computed items like net working capital and tangible net worth. The relationships are expressed as ratios and percentages and, as against the single ratio which was commonly used in the earliest years of balance sheet analysis, there are now employed over a dozen ratios for a more thorough analysis.

Current Ratio

The most important and commonly used ratio which was evolved in the earliest days of financial statement analysis is the ratio of current assets to current liabilities. Designated the "current ratio" — since it provides an indication of the "current" financial condition of a business — and frequently "working capital ratio", it shows the number of times the book-value of current assets exceeds the book-value of current liabilities. It is computed as shown in Exhibit 25 by dividing current assets by current liabilities.

Exhibit 25

POWERPACK INDIA LIMITED
Current Assets and Current Liabilities as at March 31, 20___

Amounts – Rs in Lakhs

	Year A	Year B	Year C	Year D	Year E	Year F
Current Assets						
Cash and Equivalent	85	182	266	147	245	433
Sundry Debtors	887	986	953	1075	1118	1301
Inventories	1076	983	1168	1282	1283	1311
Other Current Assets	169	178	187	162	148	195
Total Current Assets	2217	2329	2574	2666	2794	3240
Current Liabilities						
Sundry Creditors	567	598	719	690	670	761
Short-term Loans	295	310	370	360	350	400
Provisions	461	485	383	562	546	623
Other Current Liabilities	150	158	190	183	178	202
Total Current Liabilities	1473	1551	1862	1795	1744	1986
Net Working Capital	744	778	712	871	1050	1254
Net Sales	3513	4277	4779	5423	5690	6145
Quick Assets	972	1168	1219	1222	1363	1734
Finished Goods Inventories	268	160	176	278	260	212
Raw Materials Inventories	808	823	992	1004	1023	1099
Raw Materials Consumed	1999	2519	2693	3043	2814	2977

From the earliest time, a current ratio of 200 per cent, or rupees two of current assets for every rupee of current liabilities, has been considered adequate for a commercial or industrial concern. The assumption on which the "two-for-one" standard is based is that in case of bankruptcy, falling prices, or inflated figures, the book-value of current assets can shrink by one half but the creditors can still receive full payment of their dues or obligations.

But, as mentioned earlier, the amount of working capital depends on several factors and a common or standard current ratio cannot be accepted as applicable to all companies irrespective of the type of their business, and their age and size. The "two-for-one" current ratio should be taken, therefore, as a good starting point and the other ratios discussed in this and the following chapters should be computed and considered also before passing a judgement on the soundness of the current financial status of a business enterprise.

While studying the current financial condition of a firm as indicated by its current ratio, the analyst must always be watchful of signs of "window dressing", that is, efforts made to overstate current assets and understate current liabilities with a view to presenting a more favourable picture of the firm's current financial position. There are several subtle devices often employed by managements to bolster the current ratio.

Some of the ways of achieving this end are: (1) overstate the book-value of inventories, (2) postpone replenishment of inventories, (3) put pressure on customers to pay their outstanding bills before the year-end, (4) use all available cash to pay off creditors just before the annual closing of accounts, (5) record in advance cash receipts relating to the following year's sales, (6) show current year's debits as relating to the succeeding year's operations, (7) include among long-term loans or deferred liabilities debts repayable within the next twelve months, (8) transfer amounts from reserves to provisions or *vice versa,* and (9) not to make a provision for taxation, or the proposed dividend on the ground that these would be paid out of the reserves when due. While the analyst must be watchful of any attempt at window-dressing, in practice it may be extremely difficult for him to obtain the information necessary to detect it.

The current ratio indicates to some extent the "margin of safety", or the "cushion", available to current creditors. It provides a measure of the liquidity of current investments and the ability of the business to meet its maturing current obligations. In theory at any rate, therefore, the larger the current ratio the greater is the protection available to short-term creditors and the better is the debt-paying ability of the concern.

In practice, however, a company with a high current ratio may not necessarily be in a position to meet promptly its maturing obligations because, as mentioned earlier, of an improper distribution of current assets in relation to liquidity. Moreover, the current ratio is just one of several ratios each of which, in conjunction with some other ratio and other facts may have to tell a supplementary story. Further, it is a generality which all by itself possibly cannot give a clear picture of the inherent soundness or weakness of a financial position.

Quick or "Acid-test" Ratio

For a long time the "two-for-one" current ratio was the alpha and omega of balance sheet analysis and was extensively used because every-day experience had indicated its practical significance. In course of time, however, a simple supplementary ratio was evolved which compared the total of cash or its equivalent, and sundry debtors — the so-called "Quick" assets — against total current liabilities. It was called the "Quick Ratio" since it measured only the quick assets against current liabilities.

If the current ratio was two-for-one, or better, and quick assets were at least equal to current liabilities, a double assurance, so to say, was provided of the soundness of the current financial position of a business. If total current liabilities were in excess of quick assets, some doubt was thrown on the strength of the balance sheet. Thus this supplementary ratio provided what may be called the "Acid-test" of the current financial soundness of the business.

The reason why inventories and pre-paid expenses or deposits are not to be included in the computation of the quick ratio is that it normally takes time for their realisation in cash. Raw materials and work-in-progress must, first, be turned into finished goods through the process of manufacture. The goods must then be turned into sundry debtors by means of sales and the book debts must, thereafter be realised in cash. Again, inventories may include a small or large stock of old, worthless, second-rate, or immovable goods which may not be saleable at all.

The acid-test ratio represents the number of times current liabilities are covered by quick assets or the number of rupees of liquid assets relative to total current liabilities. If a company has a quick ratio of at least one hundred per cent it is considered to be in a fairly good current financial position since it is then presumed to be able to meet readily its current obligations. Care must be taken, however, not to place too much reliance on a hundred per cent quick ratio without further investigation.

Book debts in certain cases may not be readily realisable and cash may be needed to pay for emergency or immediate operating expenses. On the other hand, inventories may be more liquid than book debts. Also, the sale of inventories normally results in profits, which in turn increase the amount of working capital. Finally, it is the inventories which are available to a measurable extent to meet current liabilities because of the normal conversion of stocks of finished goods into sales and, then, into cash.

The ratios of current assets and quick assets to current liabilities of Powerpack India Ltd. for the Years A-F, inclusive, ended March 31, are given in the table below.

POWERPACK INDIA LIMITED

Current Assets and Quick Assets in Relation to Current Liabilities

Year ended Mar. 31	Current Assets Rs Lakhs	Quick Assets Rs Lakhs	Current Liabilities Rs Lakhs	Current Ratio Times	Quick Ratio %
A	2217	972	1473	1.51	66.0
B	2329	1168	1551	1.50	75.3
C	2574	1219	1862	1.38	65.5
D	2666	1222	1795	1.49	68.1
E	2794	1363	1744	1.60	78.2
F	3240	1734	1986	1.63	87.3

In none of the six years whose financial data are being analysed, was the current ratio of Powerpack India Ltd. the standard two-for-one, nor was the quick ratio one hundred per cent. The reason was that during a part of the period the company was engaged in enlarging its manufacturing facilities and was required to divert much of its cash resources towards meeting part of the capital expenditure involved.

On the one hand, this prevented Powerpack India Ltd. from building up to an adequate level the inventory of finished goods which remained in high demand. On the other hand, the company was forced to depend more heavily an creditor funds for keeping on hand an adequate stock of raw materials to maintain the level of production. In consequence, the investment in current assets remained low relative to current liabilities as well as net sales.

Ratio of Net Sales to Sundry Debtors

The total debts shown outstanding on the books of account of a company as at a particular date, depend upon the sales volume handled, the credit policy of the company, the efficiency of its bills collection department, and the effectiveness of its bills collection procedure. The more liberal are the credit terms and the less efficient is the working of the collection department, the larger will be the amount of outstanding bills for the same volume of sales.

Since sundry debtors constitute an important item of current assets, the amount of outstanding bills inclusive of bills of exchange or trade acceptances, must not exceed at any time a reasonable proportion of net sales. This relationship is expressed as a ratio computed by dividing net sales by the figure of sundry debtors as follows:

$$\frac{\text{Net Sales : Rs } 5,271 \text{ lakh}}{\text{Sundry Debtors : Rs } 910 \text{ lakh}} = 5.79 \text{ times or } 579.2 \%$$

This may be interpreted to mean that, (1) net sales are 579.2 per cent of book debts, or (2) net sales are approximately 5.79 times of sundry debtors, or (3) book debts are collected approximately 5.79 times during the year, or (4) the "turnover" of sundry debtors is 5.79 times. If a turnover of, say, four times is found to be typical of the industry, a turnover of 5.79 times is considered high and indicative of a general shortage of net working capital with consequent low investment in book debts.

Other things remaining equal, a low turnover of debtors indicates that a relatively larger portion of the working capital is invested in book debts. An increasing turnover over the years reflects stricter credit terms, a more effective collection procedure, or a relatively declining investment in sundry debtors.

It must be noted that the computation of the turnover figure is based on net sales for the year as a whole and outstanding debts for the concluding few months of the year. The ratio of net sales to sundry debtors based on the yearly figure of net sales, therefore, is likely to be somewhat overstated as compared with monthly or quarterly ratios.

Average Collection Period

The turnover of book debts divided into the number of days in the year, normally 365, gives what is known as the Average Collection Period, or the number of days of credit outstanding as at the date of the balance sheet. If the turnover ratio is 5.79 times, the average collection period works out to 63 days as follows:

$$\frac{\text{Number of Days in Year : } 365}{\text{Turnover Ratio : } 5.79 \text{ times}} = \text{Average Collection Period - 63 days.}$$

The same result can be obtained by, first, dividing total net sales by the number of days in the year to get average daily net credit sales and, then, dividing the amount of book debts by the figure of average daily net sales as follows:

$$\frac{\text{Net Sales} : \text{Rs } 5{,}271 \text{ lakh}}{\text{No. of Days in Year} : 365} = \text{Average Daily Net Sales Rs } 14{,}44{,}110 \text{ approx. or Rs } 14.44 \text{ lakh.}$$

$$\frac{\text{Sundry Debtors} : \text{Rs } 910 \text{ lakh}}{\text{Average Daily Net Sales} : \text{Rs } 14.44 \text{ lakh}} = \text{Average Age of Debtors 63 days.}$$

What the figure really means is that sundry debtors as stated on the balance sheet represent approximately 63 days credit and not 63 days credit sales. In other words, bills are collected after 63 days on an average. The figure provides a useful measure of the effectiveness of the bills collection procedure and the efficiency of the bills collection department. If it exceeds, in a significant manner, the period normally allowed to clients by the competitors, it means that the collection procedure is defective and that collections are delayed for too long.

The turnover of sundry debtors and the average collection period for Powerpack India Ltd. for the six-year period Year A to Year F, inclusive, ended March 31, are shown in the table below.

POWERPACK INDIA LIMITED
Turnover of Sundry Debtors and Average Collection Period

Year ended March 31	Net sales Rs Lakhs	Sundry Debtors Rs Lakhs	Days in the year No.	Turnover of Debtors Times	Average Collection Period Days
A	3513	887	365	3.96	92
B	4277	986	366	4.34	84
C	4779	953	365	5.01	73
D	5423	1075	365	5.04	72
E	5690	1118	365	5.09	72
F	6145	1301	366	4.72	78

For the six-year period as a whole, the turnover of debtors averaged 4.72 times while the mean average collection period was 77.3 days. It will be noted that the turnover figure increased rapidly from 3.96 times in Year A to 5.09 times in Year E but declined the next year to 4.72 times, the average for the period under review. The change in the turnover figures tell us quite something about the management's policy in regard to extension of credit to its customers.

As already mentioned, Powerpack India Ltd. was engaged during this period in the establishment of a new manufacturing unit, operations at which began to stabilise only in Year F, ended March 31.

Since, between Year A and Year D, cash resources had to be diverted to finance partly the setting up of new manufacturing facilities, there was a shortage of net working capital in relation to net sales and this, probably, necessitated a lower investment in sundry debtors. Possibly, the company tightened its credit facilities and shortened the period of credit earlier allowed to customers. This is evident from the decline in the average collection period from 92 days in Year A to 72 days in Year E.

After completing the expansion of manufacturing facilities and stabilising production to the desired extent in Year E, the company, it seems, thought it possible to relax somewhat its credit facilities. In Year F, the turnover of debtors declined to 4.72 times from 5.09 times in the previous year while the average collection period increased to 78 days from 72 days. The changes occurred because of an increase of 19.4 per cent in net working capital and of 16.4 per cent in sundry debtors as against which net sales advanced by only eight per cent.

Turnover of Inventories

The terms, "turnover of inventories" refers to the number of times in a year the stock of finished goods is "turned over", or sold and replaced. The figure is computed by dividing net sales by the year-end inventory of finished goods as shown below:

$$\frac{\text{Net sales : Rs } 4{,}972 \text{ lakh}}{\text{Closing Inventories : Rs } 1{,}184 \text{ lakh}} = \text{Turnover of Inventories } 4.20 \text{ times.}$$

Where the cost of goods sold is available, as in the case of Powerpack India Ltd., it is more appropriate to use it instead of net sales because net sales are always shown at selling prices which include the probable profit whereas closing inventories are shown at actual costs or market prices whichever are lower. The computation of the turnover figure in such cases is as follows:

$$\frac{\text{Cost of Sales : Rs } 3{,}763 \text{ lakh}}{\text{Closing Inventories : Rs } 1{,}184 \text{ lakh}} = \text{Turnover of Inventories } 3.18 \text{ times.}$$

Since, however, the figure of cost of goods sold, or cost of sales, is not available in most cases, the ratio of net sales to closing inventories of finished goods is more commonly used than the ratio of cost of goods sold to year-end inventories of finished goods. Again the net "sales-to-inventory" ratio has to be used in making comparisons with statements of companies which do not provide the figure of cost of goods sold.

Here, again, caution has to be exercised in drawing firm conclusions since the inventory represents the value of goods on hand only on the last day of the accounting year while the cost of goods sold represents the expense for the whole year. For various reasons, the year-end inventory may not be typical of the year as a whole and might have been increased in anticipation of a larger demand, or conversely, might have been reduced to a minimum because of expectation of lesser demand or lower prices or in order to place the business in a more liquid position. If possible, an average of month-end inventory figures may be used instead of the year-end figure.

The average age of inventories, that is, the average number of days inventories remain on hand, is computed by dividing the number of days in the year by the turnover of inventories as follows:

$$\frac{\text{Days in the year} : 365}{\text{Inventory Turnover} : 3.18} = \text{Average Age of Inventories 114.8 days}$$

A high inventory turnover indicates a relatively lower investment of working capital in inventories. A low turnover indicates dull business conditions, over-investment in inventories relative to net sales, or accumulation of absolute and unsaleable goods. Whether the turnover is high, normal, or low is to be decided by comparison with similar turnover figures for the preceding periods, or those of the nearest competitor or the industry average.

The turnover and average age of finished goods inventories of Powerpack India Ltd. for the six-years, A-F, inclusive, ended March 31, are presented in the following table

POWERPACK INDIA LIMITED
Turnover and Average Age of Finished Goods Inventories

Year Ended Mar. 31	Net Sales Rs Lakhs	Inventories Rs Lakhs	Days in a year No.	Turnover of Inventories Times	Average Age of Inventories Days
A	3513	268	365	13.11	28
B	4277	160	366	26.73	14
C	4779	176	365	27.15	13
D	5423	278	365	19.51	19
E	5690	260	365	21.88	17
F	6415	213	365	28.85	13

It will be noted that the closing value of finished goods stock had been low in relation to net sales and had averaged Rs 226 lakh against average net sales of Rs 4,971 lakh for the six-year period as a whole. The average turnover had been 22 times and the average age of inventories as short as 17 days. This had been the case because of the strong market demand for batteries which Powerpack India was unable to meet owing to production shortfalls resulting from labour problems.

If total inventories (raw materials, work-in-progress and finished goods) are employed in the calculations instead of closing inventories of only finished goods, the picture presented will be somewhat different as in the following table:

POWERPACK INDIA LIMITED

Turnover and Average Age of Total Inventories

Year ended Mar. 31	Net Sales Rs Lakhs	Inventories Rs Lakhs	Days in a year No.	Turnover of Inventories Times	Average Age Inventories Days
A	3513	1076	365	3.26	112
B	4277	983	366	4.35	84
C	4779	1168	365	4.09	89
D	5423	1282	365	4.23	86
E	5690	1283	365	4.43	82
F	6145	1311	366	4.69	78

The picture is more reassuring in that, the average turnover of total inventories has been a reasonable 4.20 times during a year and the average age of such inventories 87 days. The company has not been finding itself as short of essential raw materials for production as of finished goods for sale.

To find out whether the company has been over-stocking raw materials compared to actual consumption, the following ratios may be computed and compared with similar figures for other companies in the same line of business:

1. $\dfrac{\text{Raw Materials Consumed}}{\text{Raw materials Inventory}}$ = Raw Materials Turnover

2. $\dfrac{\text{Number of Days in Year}}{\text{Raw Materials Turnover}}$ = Average Age of Raw Materials Inventory

The turnover of raw materials and the average age of raw material inventories of Powerpack India Ltd. for each of the six years A-F, ended March 31, are given in the table on next page.

POWERPACK INDIA LIMITED

Turnover and Average Age of Raw Material Inventories

Year Ended Mar. 31	Raw Materials Consumed Rs Lakhs	Raw Materials Inventories Rs Lakhs	Days in a Year No.	Turnover of Raw Materials Inventories Times	Average Age of Raw Materials Inventories Days
A	1999	808	365	2.47	148
B	2519	823	366	3.06	120
C	2693	992	365	2.71	135
D	3043	1004	365	3.03	120
E	2814	1023	365	2.75	133
F	2977	1099	366	2.71	135

For the six-year period under study, Powerpack India Ltd. had consumed each year raw materials worth Rs 2,674 lakh on an average and the average value of closing inventories of raw materials and work-in-progress had been Rs 958 lakh. Thus, the average turnover of inventories had been 2.79 times during a year and the average age of inventories 131 days. By comparing these figures with those of other companies or the industry average, an over-investment or an under-investment in raw materials inventories may be detected.

Ratio of Inventories to Net Working Capital

It will be noted from the foregoing that the relationship between net sales, or cost of goods sold to inventories is between two items which often change considerably from one year to another. Obviously, if both the items increase or decrease in the same proportion, the ratio remains unchanged. But this rarely happens as can be noticed from the data of Powerpack India Ltd. given earlier.

If the upward trend in net sales and inventories continues year after year, it is but natural that, at some stage, inventories must become excessive for the size of the business, that is in relation to tangible net worth if not in relation to net sales.

If, for some reason, there is a sudden drop in inventory values, a loss is suffered which may wipe out a part of the net working capital and also the net worth. Again, if net working capital remains unchanged, or fails to grow in line with net sales and the supporting inventories, a larger inventory build-up is possible only by the use of an excessive amount of current credit. If there is a decline in net sales due to unforeseen circumstances, sufficient funds may not be realised through sales to repay current borrowings when due and the business may find itself in a vulnerable financial position.

There is need, therefore, to supplement the ratio of net sales to inventories by another to reveal the possibility of such a situation developing. This ratio measures the relationship between a variable, inventories of finished goods, and net working capital, an item which changes very modestly from one year to another. The ratio, thus, provides a more stable basis for comparison than is supplied by the figure of turnover of inventories.

The following table presents the ratio of inventories to net working capital and the ratio of net sales to net working capital, that is, the turnover of net working capital of Powerpack India Ltd. for the period ended March 31, Year A to Year F, inclusive.

POWERPACK INDIA LIMITED

**Ratio of Total Inventories to Net Sales & Turnover
of Net Working Capital**

Year Ended Mar. 31	Net Sales Rs Lakhs	Total Inventories Rs Lakhs	Net Working Capital Rs Lakhs	Ratio to Net Working Capital of	
				Net Sales Times	Inventories %
A	3513	1076	744	4.72	144.6
B	4277	983	778	5.50	126.3
C	4779	1168	712	6.71	164.0
D	5423	1282	871	6.23	147.2
E	5690	1283	1050	5.42	122.2
F	6145	1311	1254	4.90	104.5

As a rule, for large manufacturers or wholesalers, inventories should not exceed net working capital if financial difficulties and worries are to be avoided. In the case of Powerpack India Ltd., the ratio of total inventories to net working capital has always exceeded 100 per cent in each of the six years A to F though, since Year D the percentage has declined rapidly to 104.5 from 164.0 in Year C.

Ratio of Net Sales to Net Working Capital or Turnover of Net Working Capital

An obvious relationship exists between net sales and net working capital. As the sales volumes expand, larger inventories are required to he carried to sustain sales and sundry debtors also show a rising trend. In other words, a larger net working capital becomes necessary. To measure the adequacy of net working capital in relation to projected sales and to test the efficiency of use of net working capital, it is customary in financial statement analysis to compute the "turnover of net working capital" by dividing net sales by net working capital thus:

$$\frac{\text{Net Sales : Rs 4,410 lakh}}{\text{Net Working Capitals : Rs 752 Lakh}} = \text{Turnover of Net Working Capital - 5.86 times.}$$

Whether or not a turnover of 5.86 times is high is to be determined by comparison with the turnover figures for the company for prior years or with those of other competing companies or the industry average.

A high turnover of net working capital at times reflects a more efficient use of capital, but more often it indicates a shortage of net working capital owing to over-investment in fixed assets and heavier current liabilities which may mature for payment before both inventories and book debts can be converted into cash. It is often the result of overtrading, permanent or temporary, and may indicate the need to cut down the sales volume or to introduce into the business additional permanent capital or long-term borrowings.

A low turnover of net working capital may be due to under-trading, excess of net working capital, a slow turnover of inventories and sundry debtors, or a large cash balance temporarily invested in readily marketable securities as often happens after an issue of shares or debentures to finance an expansion.

In the case of Powerpack India Ltd., the turnover of net working capital steadily rose till Year C but later declined to 4.90 in the concluding year of the period under review. As earlier stated, the company had to divert much of its cash resource to finance the setting-up of new manufacturing facilities and had been short of the net working capital needed to support an expanding volume of sales. The new productive capacity went on stream in Year D and, with more cash funds becoming untied, there took place a perceptible increase in net working capital.

Interpretation

Having analysed the data at his disposal and having computed the different ratios and percentage discussed in earlier paragraphs, the analyst must interpret the results of his analysis. He must draw logical conclusions regarding the current financial position of the company during the period under study and, if possible, comment on the short-term financial policy the company has been following in pursuit of set objectives. Not being privy to inside information, his conclusions may not turn out to be precise. But, depending upon his experience, these can be sufficiently accurate.

Working Capital Ratios — Illustration

Powerpack India Limited

Using the data made available by the balance sheets of Powerpack India Ltd. as at March 31, for the Years A through F, the following broad conclusions can be drawn about the current financial status of the company based on the assumption that year-end figures of assets and liabilities are typical of the year, that is, close to their monthly averages and that there has been no attempt at window-dressing.

1. Powerpack India Ltd. is the largest and leading manufacturer of a wide range of models of a vital component of the engine of all types of transport equipment driven by petrol and diesel oil. The reputation of its products is so well-established that the demand for them has always well exceeded their production even at full capacity utilisation.

2. With a view to meeting this demand more effectively the company planned an expansion of capacity. The work on the project commenced in Year A and was completed during Year D. However, it was not till Year F, that the initial teething troubles could be overcome and production could be stabilised at the desired level.

3. To finance the capital expenditure involved, the company first, raised a long-term loan by issuing non-convertible debentures and, then, doubled the equity capital through a rights issue. Even then, the company felt the need, at least during the first half of the six-year period under review, to divert some of its current earnings towards capital spending.

This prevented it from strengthening its current financial position to the extent possible and forced it to rely more heavily on creditor finance. This is evident from the fact that in none of the six years under consideration, was its current ratio the standard two-for-one nor was the quick ratio one hundred per cent of current liabilities.

4. The company seemingly did not experience shortage of net working capital to support the volume of business it was handling since the annual turnover of net working capital (measured by the ratio of net sales to net working capital) averaged 4.8 times for the period as a whole. This, however, was for two reasons.

First, as will be explained in the next chapter, the average annual sales themselves were low in relation to the tangible net worth of the business, that is the amount of funds contributed by the shareholders.

Second, having an easier access to creditor funds, the company had invested far too heavily in raw materials inventories than it would have had its own funds been at stake. Speaking of the six-year period as a whole, raw materials claimed as much as eighty-one per cent of the total funds sunk in inventories leaving only nineteen per cent for finished goods stock on hand.

5. The rate of turnover of inventories defines the number of times during a year raw material stocks are consumed in production and replaced. For Powerpack India Ltd., the turnover was as low as 2.8 times a year on the average and, at any date, the company held in stock raw materials enough to meet manufacturing requirements for as many as 131 days.

6. As against this, the average turnover of finished goods inventories was as high as nineteen times and the average age of finished goods inventories, too, was nineteen days. The faster-than-normal turnover and all-too-short average age of finished goods inventories were no doubt indicative of the reputation and demand for Powerpack India's range of products enjoyed in the market. But, the facts also underscored the low investment the company could make in finished goods inventories owing to an overall shortage of own funds.

CHAPTER 22

Analysis of Long-term Financial Condition

The balance sheet of every company, as was shown in Chapter 2, is broadly divisible on the assets as well as the liabilities side into two parts, the one comprising current items of assets and liabilities and the other non-current or long-term items. The composition of current assets, their relationship with current liabilities, and ratio analysis of net working capital all throw light on the current or short-term financial standing of the firm with which the company's bankers and trade creditors are intimately connected.

Term-lending institutions, bondholders, shareholders or owners and, of course, employees are most interested in the firm's continued ability to meet its debt repayment obligations, to conduct its operations profitably, to maintain the stream of future dividends, and to finance expansion and diversification of its activities as far as possible without raising additional share capital or long-term loans.

The two divisions of the balance sheet are not water-tight however, and changes taking place in the one part are bound to be reflected in the situation now prevailing in the other. Thus a favourable current position is invariably affected by a steady deterioration in the long-term financial condition of the business and, in the same ways a favourable long-term financial position may get affected by a persistent deterioration in the firm's current financial standing. In the like manner, any improvement over the years in the current situation will eventually help the long-term financial condition to improve, and an improvement in a currently weak long-term position will go to further strengthen the current financial situation.

For instance, a company enjoying a strong current position will have adequate working capital with balanced investment in book debts and inventories, and only moderately heavy current obligations. But, it may have a weak long-term financial condition with over-investment in fixed assets financed by excessive borrowings. The interest payable on these may squeeze the profit margin and make debt repayment and accretion to working capital difficult.

In the contrary situation a firm may have a balanced capital structure comprising the owners' equity and long-term loans and with no more than an adequate investment in fixed assets. Yet, it may find itself regularly short of net working capital because of over-investment in sundry debtors or in inventories purchased by making excessive use of creditor funds.

In the former case the situation can be improved only by raising additional share capital to repay term loans and release the profit margin from the interest payment burden. To rectify the situation described in the latter case, the company will have to take quick measures to recover dues from its customers or to reduce over-investment in inventories whichever happens to be the case.

What is being stressed here is simply this that, neither of the two groups interested in a company's financial status can logically ignore the aspect of primary interest to the other and must concern itself with both the current and non-current sections of the balance sheets to locate the favourable and unfavourahle trends tending to emerge.

Illustration — Powerpack India Limited

The point is well illustrated by the case of Powerpack India Ltd. whose short-term financial status was analysed in the previous chapter. During the five year period, March 31 Year A to March 31 Year F, the company was engaged in enlarging its productive capacity with the view to meeting effectively the growing demand for its range of products. To finance the cost of expansion not only did the company have to make an issue of non-convertible debentures during Year C and an issue of rights equity shares in Year F, but was also obliged to divert a portion of its current cash generation to meet capital expenditure.

The long-term finance introduced during the five year period was Rs 1,685 lakh as shown in Exhibit 26 and was made up of:

Increase in Share Capital	Rs 646 lakh
Increase in Reserves	Rs 371 lakh
Increase In Term Loans	Rs 264 lakh
Increase in Depreciation written off fixed Assets	Rs 404 lakh
Total Sources	Rs 1,685 lakh
These funds were utilised in the following manner:	
Investment in Fixed Assets Gross	Rs 1,054 lakh
Investment in Non-current	
Assets – Net	Rs 121 lakh
Increase in Net Working Capital	Rs 510 lakh
Total Applications	Rs 1,685 lakh

It will be noted from the analysis in Exhibit 26 that the introduction of additional funds in the business helped Powerpack India Ltd. not only to strengthen its long-term financial position but to bring about some favourable changes in its current or short-term financial status as well.

As a result of the issuance of rights equity shares and the continued plough-back of profits, the percentage of owners' equity in the total of liabilities and net worth improved to 49.2 from 44 five year earlier. Similarly, the percentage of net fixed assets in the total of all assets almost doubled from 11.2 to 21. These changes were favourable from the point of view of providers of long-term credit.

The introduction of additional long-term finance also seems to have helped the company to some extent to reduce dependence on creditor funds for its working capital requirements. As will be seen from Powerpack India's summarised balance sheet presented as Exhibit 27, net sales advanced by 74.9 per cent from Rs 3,513 lakh in Year A ended March 31, to Rs 6,145 lakh in Year F, but current liabilities increased by only 34.8 per cent. This was the outcome perhaps of relatively lower investment in current assets which, as at the end of Year F formed 73.2 per cent of total assets as against 84.1 per cent as at the end of Year A as shown in Exhibit 26.

In absolute rupee amounts however, current assets increased over the five-year period by Rs 1,023 lakh or 46.1 per cent but the increase in current liabilities was lower at Rs 513 lakh or 34.8 per cent. These changes are favourable from the point of view of short-term creditors being indicative of increased investment by the owners in the net working capital of the business which reveals a growth of Rs 510 lakh.

Ratio Analysis of Long-term Financial Condition

What the foregoing discussion brings out is that changes in the long-term financial standing of a business can, and often do, bring about corresponding changes in the short-term or current financial condition as well. By the same token, changes in the short-term financial situation can induce changes in the long-term condition. It cannot be gainsaid, nevertheless, that a favourable change in one situation will not induce a contrary change in the other.

To be able to conclude, therefore, that the changes in the financial position taking place are favourable or otherwise, both from the long-term as well as the short-term point of view, the analyst should undertake ratio analysis of the non-current items on the balance sheet along with ratio analysis of net working capital explained in the preceding chapter.

Ratios of Current and Total Liabilities to Tangible Net Worth

The relationship between liabilities (borrowed funds) and net worth (own funds) or owners' equity, has implications significant to both the

Exhibit 26

POWERPACK INDIA LIMITED

Investment in Assets and Source of Funds as at March 31, Year A and Year F

Items	Year A Amount Rs Lakhs	Year A %	Year F Amount Rs Lakhs	Year F %	Increases of Decreases (D) Amount Rs Lakhs	Increases of Decreases (D) %
ASSETS						
Current Assets	2217	84.1	3240	73.2	1023	46.1
Non-Current Assets	126	4.7	242	5.5	116	92.1
Fixed Assets – Gross	767	29.1	1821	41.1	1054	137.4
Less : Depreciation	472	17.9	876	19.8	404	85.6
Fixed Assets – Net	295	11.2	945	21.3	650	220.3
TOTAL ASSETS	2638	100.0	4427	100.0	1789	67.8
BORROWED FUNDS						
Current Liabilities	1473	55.8	1986	44.9	513	34.8
Non-Current Liabilities	5	0.2	-	-	5 (D)	100.0 (D)
Long-term Loans	-	-	264	5.9	264	-
TOTAL LIABILITIES	1478	56.0	2250	50.8	772	52.0

Contd....

Exhibit 26 (Contd...)

POWERPACK INDIA LIMITED

Investment in Assets and Source of Funds as at March 31, Year A and Year F

Items	Year A		Year F		Increases of Decreases	
	Amount Rs Lakhs	%	Amount Rs Lakhs	%	Amount Rs Lakhs	%
NET WORTH						
Equity Share Capital	645	24.5	1291	29.2	646	100.2
Reserves	515	19.5	886	20.0	371	72.0
TOTAL NET WORTH	1160	44.0	2177	49.2	1017	87.7
TOTAL LIABILITIES AND NET WORTH	2638	100.0	4427	100.0	1789	67.8

Exhibit 27

POWERPACK INDIA LIMITED
Summarised Balance Sheet as at March 31, 20___

Amounts – Rs in Lakhs

	Year A	Year B	Year C	Year D	Year E	Year F
ASSETS						
Current Assets	2217	2329	2574	2666	2794	3240
Miscellaneous Assets	126	153	178	198	229	242
Fixed Assets – Net	295	417	642	859	944	945
Total Assets	2638	2899	3394	3723	3967	4427
LIABILITIES AND NET WORTH						
a. Liabilities						
Current Liabilities	1473	1551	1862	1795	1744	1986
Deferred Liabilities	5	-	5	4	2	-
Long-term Loans	-	108	132	248	296	264
Total Liabilities	1478	1659	1999	2047	2042	2250
b. Tangible Net Worth						
Share Capital	645	645	645	968	1129	1290
Reserves	515	595	750	708	796	887
Total Tangible Net Worth	1160	1240	1395	1676	1925	2177
Total Liabilities and Tangible Net Worth	2638	2899	3394	3723	3967	4427
c. Net Sale	3513	4277	4779	5423	5690	6145
d. Net Profit	223	253	348	475	496	536

owners and the creditors of a business. From the point of view of the owners, a larger amount of contributed capital and retained profits relieves the profit margin of the business from the pressure of interest payable on the borrowed funds besides rendering it less dependent in its day-to-day operations on the attitude of its creditors.

From the point of view of the creditors, the larger the amount of funds contributed by the owners, the wider is the margin of safety, or "cushion", available to them. This mutuality of interest of the owners and the long- and short-term creditors of the business has been long recognised by serious students of financial statements, and ratios have been evolved to measure the relationship between the tangible net worth and (1) current liabilities, and (2) total liabilities to outsiders.

The evolution of two distinct ratios to measure the relationship between the funds contributed by the owners of a business and those provided by creditors, has a historical background. When in the distant past, the concept first arose that a typical commercial or industrial business enterprise should not have liabilities in excess of the capital supplied by the owners, few concerns had long-term liabilities in the form of term-loans and debenture bonds. For the majority of business enterprises, therefore, liabilities were synonymous with what are now known as current liabilities.

In this situation a concept developed that creditors, for the sake of the safety of their own capital, should have no more funds at stake in a business than the owners themselves had and the first of the two ratios mentioned was evolved.

The situation has changed significantly with the increasing use now being made of long-term loans, through the issue of debenture bonds or otherwise, as an instrument of financing business ventures and a degree of analytical specialisation has become essential.

It has come to be realised that between two enterprises with the same amount of total liabilities, the one with modest current liabilities, but with a substantial long-term loan due payable ten or more years in the future, would be a far better risk for current creditors than the one with no "term" loan outstanding but with a large current liability. This realisation has led to the evolution of the second ratio, that is, the ratio of total liabilities to tangible net worth.

The two ratios are computed by dividing respectfully (1) current liabilities, and (2) total liabilities consisting of all current liabilities together with all actual long-term liabilities, by tangible net worth and expressing the quotient as a percentage as shown in the table on next page for Powerpack India Ltd.

POWERPACK INDIA LIMITED

Ratios of Current Liabilities and Total Liabilities to Tangible Net Worth

Year ended Mar. 31	Tangible Net Worth Rs lakhs	Current Liabilities Rs lakhs	Total Liabilities Rs lakhs	Ratio to Tangible Net Worth of	
				Current Liabilities %	Total Liabilities %
A	1160	1473	1478	127.0	127.4
B	1240	1551	1659	125.1	133.8
C	1395	1862	1999	133.5	143.3
D	1676	1795	2047	107.1	122.1
E	1925	1744	2042	90.6	106.1
F	2177	1986	2250	91.2	103.4

The ratio of current liabilities to tangible net worth compares the funds creditors temporarily have at risk in a concern in the form of business debts with the funds permanently invested by the owners. The orthodox view, which emerged in the United States some time during the last quarter of the nineteenth century is that, a typical commercial or industrial business enterprise should not have current liabilities in excess of the invested capital, that is its net worth. From the point of view of short-term creditors this means that they, for their own protection, should have no more funds at stake in a particular venture than the owners of that enterprise themselves have.

If current liabilities exceed, or form a high percentage of tangible net worth, as in the case of Powerpack India Ltd., it usually means that the concern is "overtrading", that is, handling a volume of business which is large in relation to its net working capital and its tangible net worth.

Overtrading will not necessarily lead to disastrous consequences if the management of a business is in experienced hands and the market for its products is established and growing. But, the situation might become critical if prices were to suddenly fall or if it were to become difficult to collect dues from customers.

The ratio of total liabilities to tangible net worth compares the respective interests of the owners or proprietors of a business on the one hand, and that of outside creditors on other. Theoretically the greater the interest of the owners the more satisfactory is the financial structure of the business because in such a situation the management is less handicapped by the attitude of the creditors, and the less heavy is the burden of interest charges and debt repayment requirements.

As said earlier, however, almost all large businesses depend on borrowed funds (term-loans from lending institutions and debenture bonds) to finance their undertakings and it is difficult to determine the most appropriate balance between borrowed funds and owners' equity. If a minimum amount of borrowed funds is used, the ratio between total liabilities and tangible net worth would ordinarily reflect "too-safe" a position. On the other hand, extensive use of long-term borrowings would usually reveal a dangerous situation.

Interpretation of the ratio, therefore, depends almost entirely on the type of business, its future prospects, the quality of its management, and the financial and business policies of the enterprise. A company which has a stable profit or has an experienced and successful management, can afford to operate on a maximum amount of borrowed funds.

For a company with an unstable profit record, or one operating within a cyclical industry, a high ratio of total liabilities to owners' equity reflects a speculative situation. In periods of prosperity, fixed interest charges may claim a smaller proportion of the profit and leave a comparatively larger surplus for the owners. In periods of depression, the business may not be able to earn the fixed interest charges or may not be able to refinance maturing obligations on favourable terms.

Ratio of Fixed Assets to Tangible Net Worth

The ratio of fixed assets to tangible net worth is determined, as in the case of Powerpack India Ltd. below, by dividing the depreciated value of fixed assets by tangible net worth.

POWERPACK INDIA LIMITED

Ratio of Net Fixed Assets to Tangible Net Worth and Long-term Loans

Year ended Mar. 31	Net Fixed Assets Rs Lakhs	Tangible Net Worth Rs Lakhs	Long-term Loans Rs Lakhs	Ratio of fixed Assets to	
				Tangible Net Worth %	Long-term Loans %
A	295	1160	—	25.4	—
B	417	1240	108	33.6	386.1
C	642	1395	132	46.0	486.4
D	859	1676	248	51.3	346.4
E	944	1925	296	49.0	318.9
F	945	2177	264	43.4	358.0

In the natural course of business the value of the depreciated block shows a downward tendency from year to year if the annual depreciation charge exceeds the amount of fresh investment in fixed assets. It is only when a costly asset is scrapped, or a factory is sold, that there is a sudden fall in the value of the depreciated block; and only when substantial expansion is undertaken, or a new factory is built, that there is a sudden rise in the value of net fixed assets.

In contrast, the tangible net worth of a business increases only gradually as a portion of the operating profit is reinvested. There will be sudden decrease only if a big loss is suffered or when preference share capital, if any, is redeemed. A large non-operating profit or an issue of additional equity shares, on the other hand, will bring about a sudden increase in tangible net worth.

The ratio of fixed assets to tangible net worth indicates the proportion of own funds to the total of funds invested in fixed assets. When the ratio is below one hundred per cent, the full value of the depreciated block as well as a portion of the working capital — assuming that there are no non-current assets — is supplied by the owners. If the ratio exceeds one hundred per cent, there is over-investment in fixed assets financed partly by long-term borrowings or creditor funds.

An over-investment in fixed assets relative to tangible net worth is unfavourable from the point of view of the annual depreciation charge which tends to depress the gross margin on sales. If it has been accomplished by making use of profits from current operations, there may result a shortage of working capital. If long-term loans are raised, either to finance investment in fixed assets or to augment net working capital, the cost of borrowing, that is, the amount of interest payable, may prove burdensome.

The data of Powerpack India Ltd. show that between March 31, Year A and Year D, tangible net worth increased by Rs 516 lakh or 44.5 per cent, but the value of the depreciated block rose faster by 191.2 per cent, or Rs 564 lakh, absorbing 51.3 per cent of the owners' equity as compared with just 25.4 per cent as at March 31, Year A.

The relatively larger investment in fixed assets was financed partly by making use of a portion of current earnings and partly by raising long-term loans through an issue of non-convertible debentures. This unfavourable trend was reversed in the next two years when the tangible net worth increased by Rs 501 lakh but the value of the depreciated block increased by only Rs 86 lakh. This resulted in the lowering of the ratio of fixed assets to tangible net worth from 51.3 per cent to 43.4 per cent, in reducing long-term loans and strengthening net working capital.

Ratio of Fixed Assets to Long-term Liabilities

This supplementary ratio reveals the security available to long-term creditors when the loans are secured by a mortgage on the fixed assets, and indicates to some extent whether or not additional loans can he raised by offering the same security. The computation of the ratio for Powerpack India Ltd. is shown in the table presented earlier.

Ratio of Tangible Net Worth to Total Assets

The ratio of tangible net worth to total assets is often called the "Proprietory Ratio" and shows the percentage of total investment in assets that has been financed by the owners or shareholders. It is computed, as shown for Powerpack India Ltd. in the table below, by dividing tangible net worth by total assets and expressing the resulting relationship as a percentage.

POWERPACK INDIA LIMITED

Ratio of Tangible Net Worth to Total Assets or Proprietary Ratio

Year Ended Mar. 31	Tangible Net Worth Rs Lakhs	Total Assets Rs Lakhs	Proprietary Ratio %	Creditor's Interest %
A	1160	2638	44.0	56.0
B	1240	2899	42.8	57.2
C	1395	3394	41.1	58.9
D	1676	3723	45.0	55.0
E	1925	3968	48.5	51.5
F	2177	4427	49.2	50.8

The difference between one hundred per cent and the proprietary ratio represents the relationship between total liabilities and total assets, that is the percentage of the investment in total assets financed by creditors. The ratio of tangible net worth to total assets and the ratio of total liabilities to total assets are thus complementary and reflect the relative importance of the owners' equity and borrowed funds in the capital invested in the business and margin of safety available to the creditors. Being so, the proprietary ratio is as important in the analysis of the long-term financial condition of a business as is the current ratio in the analysis of the firms current financial status.

The data presented in the table above reveal that throughout the six year period, Powerpack India Ltd. had depended more heavily on trade creditors than its owners for the expansion of its establishment, though, after Year C the owners' contribution had been rising steadily. This trend was favourable provided it continued after Year F.

It is obvious that at no time can the ratio of tangible net worth to total assets exceed one hundred per cent and can equal one hundred per cent provided there are no outside liabilities current or long-term. In a general sense, therefore, the closer the proprietary ratio approximates one hundred per cent, the stronger the financial position of the firm can be said to be and the better its credit rating because of the wider margin of safety available to creditors.

But, a high percentage of tangible net worth in the total funds invested in the business is not always the most profitable situation. As was explained in Chapter 8, there is a certain advantage accruing to the shareholders from "Trading on the Equity" or making use of borrowed funds provided this is kept within limits. A high proprietary ratio would, then, simply indicate insufficient use being made of readily available creditor funds to finance business operations.

A high proprietary ratio is frequently indicative of over-capitalisation and an excessive investment in current and fixed assets in relation to actual needs. There will be either an excess of working capital or a heavier investment in fixed assets than necessary for economical operations. A proprietary ratio nearing one hundred per cent is often reflected in low earnings per share and, consequently, a low rate of dividend to shareholders.

A low proprietary ratio, on the other hand, is indicative of under-capitalisation and an excessive use of creditor funds. Larger returns on the tangible net worth and the equity share capital, the latter allowing payment of large dividends, may make under-capitalisation appear desirable. But, the situation is speculative because it makes for high profits in good years and heavy losses in lean ones.

Ratio of Net Sales to Tangible Net Worth

Every business enterprise is equipped financially to undertake a certain optimum volume of sales turnover without drawing upon creditor or borrowed funds. The level of activity actually attained is measured by the ratio of net sales to tangible net worth. Also referred to as the turnover of tangible net worth, it measures the amount of sales realisation achieved for every rupee of capital invested by the owners in the business as follows.

$$\frac{\text{Net Sales : Rs 4,410 Lakh}}{\text{Tangible Net Worth : Rs 3,877 Lakh}} = \text{Net Sales per Rupee of Tangible Net Worth : Rs 1.14}$$

Whether this is high, low, or normal is to be judged by comparison with the ratio of the nearest competitor or with the industry average.

A high ratio may indicate an excessive volume of trading on a thin margin of invested or permanent capital and the consequent overuse of credit. This is described as "overtrading", that is, the process of handling a larger volume of net sales in relation to tangible net worth when compared with other companies in the same industry or line of business.

At the other end, net sales are too small in relation to tangible net worth. The ratio of net sales to tangible net worth is low and indicates a slower turnover of the contributed capital and excessive investment in fixed assets relative to net sales. This is termed "understanding", that is, handling a smaller volume of net sales than companies of a comparable size in the same industry or business.

For Powerpack India Ltd., the ratio of net sales to tangible net worth averaged 311.6 per cent for the six year period ended March 31, Year A through Year F. This is the same as to say that, net sales during the six-year period averaged Rs 3.12 per rupee of tangible net worth as shown in the following table

POWERPACK INDIA LIMITED

Ratios of Net Sales and Net Profit to Tangible Net Worth

Year ended Mar. 31	Net Sales Rs Lakhs	Net Profit Rs Lakhs	Tangible Net Worth Rs Lakhs	Ratio to Tangible Net worth of	
				Net Sales Rs	Net Profit %
A	3513	223	1160	3.03	19.2
B	4277	253	1240	3.45	20.4
C	4779	348	1395	3.43	25.0
D	5423	475	1676	3.24	28.3
E	5690	496	1925	2.96	25.8
F	6145	536	2177	2.82	24.6

Ratio of Net Profit to Tangible Net Worth

The realisation of a satisfactory return on the funds invested is the immediate objective of a business. This return is called net profit and represents the balance which remains when all of the expenses of the business for a period including extraordinary losses and income tax are deducted from the total income for that period inclusive of extraordinary gains.

There are two widely used measures of net profit — (1) a comparison with tangible net worth of a business enterprise, and (2) a comparison with net sales. While the ratio of net profit to net sales (this is discussed in the next chapter) serves as a measure of the profitability of undertaking particular operations and is more often used by active managements, the ratio of net profit to tangible net worth provides a measure of the profitable use of the funds invested in the business and the ability of the management to earn a satisfactory return on the capital employed.

A low ratio of net profit to tangible net worth may indicate that the business is not very successful because of inefficient and ineffective management, unfavourable business conditions, and excessive investment in fixed assets. A high ratio of net profit to tangible net worth may be indicative of efficient management throughout the company's organisation, favourable business conditions, and trading on the equity.

CHAPTER 23

Analysis of Income, Costs, and Profit

The fundamental soundness of a business enterprise is revealed by its balance sheet which, while presenting the firm's financial standing provides a measure of its ability to meet maturing liabilities. It is a "static" document, however, since it presents only a snapshot picture of the firm's financial standing as at a particular date and values its assets and liabilities at historical costs which may or may not have any relevance to prevailing market conditions.

A more "dynamic" statement is the profit and loss account which shows how the company is performing financially in given market conditions. It provides a more effective analysis of the economic conditions affecting the company's business and, therefore, constitutes a better guide to the future profitableness of its operations.

To the analyst who must use all of the information he can possibly obtain, both the balance sheet and the profit and loss account are, no doubt, important. But, if he were forced to choose one statement or the other, most probably he would prefer a properly prepared and detailed profit and loss account.

This is so because of the greater emphasis that, now-a-days, is being placed on earnings as compared with the book value of the assets. A company as a going concern is supposed to earn profits for its members.

The book value of its various assets such as plant and machinery, long-term investments, book debts and inventories is useless unless it can be related to the earning power of those assets, that is, the amount of profit or revenue that can be realised on them during the course of the company's future operations.

Shareholders who look forward to receiving dividend on their share holding and holders of debenture bonds who are interested in receiving regular interest and capital repayment at maturity, naturally pay more attention to the company's earning power as revealed by its profit and loss account.

Suppliers of goods and commercial banks extending short-term credit, no doubt, pay greater attention to the company's current financial position. But, even for them, the profit and loss account and not the balance sheet constitutes a more reliable guide to the company's ability to repay its debts in the future since such repayments must come out of future profits.

A detailed analysis of the profit and loss account is, therefore, of utmost importance to all concerned, may they be short-term creditors, bondholders, shareholders, managers of the business, or its directors. An analysis of the profit and loss account for a single year or period of time is not sufficiently informative, however, because normal operating conditions might not have prevailed during that period and there might have been extraordinary gains or losses which may distort the true operating profit picture.

The profit and loss account for a number of successive years should be analysed to determine and study the trends in gross and net sales, cost of goods sold, gross margin, operating and non-operating income, and the final net profit or loss, both before and after the income tax payable. For an analysis in depth, the relation to net sales of particular items of expenditure, such as advertising and sales promotion expenses, repairs and maintenance costs as well as the annual depreciation charges, should also be computed and studied.

Ratio of Cost of Goods Sold to Net Sales

The ratio of cost of goods sold to net sales is computed by dividing the cost of sales by net sales and expressing the result as a percentage. It provides a measure of the portion of the net sales income used up in producing the goods offered for sale. The difference between net sales and cost of goods sold represents the gross margin on sales. The margin should be wide enough to cover all operating expenses and interest charges and leave a balance for distribution to preference and equity shareholders.

An increase in the cost of goods sold will, obviously, narrow down the gross margin, and a decrease in the cost of goods sold will widen it. An increase in the gross margin may be brought about by (1) increasing production through more efficient utilisation of the same productive facilities and enlarging the physical volume of sales, (2) raising selling prices, (3) reducing costs, and (4) varying the product mix to produce those items which yield the largest profit.

If a company manufactures a single product, or if the cost data for all the products manufactured is separately available, it is possible to construct a statement showing the variation in the gross margin brought about by the individual factors mentioned above. In most cases, however, such detailed information is not available to the external analyst.

The rupee and trend data for sales, cost of goods sold, operating expenses, operating income, net profit and operating assets of Powerpack India Ltd., for the years A through F, ended March 31, are presented in Exhibit 28. It will be noticed that while net sales increased

Exhibit 28

POWERPACK INDIA LIMITED

Comparative Profit and Loss Account for the Years A-F ended March 31

	Year A	Year B	Year C	Year D	Year E	Year F
						Rupees in Lakhs
Net Sales	3513	4277	4779	5423	5690	6145
Cost of Goods Sold	2662	3466	3691	4092	4183	4484
Gross Margin on Sales	851	811	1088	1331	1507	1661
Operating Expenses	182	202	237	267	290	338
Operating Income	669	609	851	1064	1217	1323
Net Profit After Tax	223	253	348	475	496	536
Operating Assets – Net	295	417	642	859	944	945
			TREND PERCENTAGES			
Net Sales	100	122	136	154	162	175
Cost of Goods Sold	100	130	139	154	157	168
Gross Margin on Sales	100	95	128	156	177	195
Operating Expenses	100	111	130	147	159	186
Operating Income	100	91	127	159	182	198
Net Profit After Tax	100	113	156	213	222	240
Operating Assets – Net	100	141	218	291	320	320

during the period by 75 per cent from Rs 3,513 lakh in Year A to Rs 6,145 lakh in Year F, cost of goods sold increased by only 68 per cent and, hence, the gross margin could widen by 95 per cent.

The reason, as can be seen from the table below, was that while in Year A, cost of goods sold claimed 75.8 per cent of net sales and 81 per cent the next year, it subsequently absorbed successively smaller amounts and in Year F formed only 73 per cent of net sales. Gross margin which was 24.2 per cent of net sales in Year A and 19 per cent in Year B, gradually increased to represent 27 per cent of net sales. For the period as a whole, the proportion of cost of goods sold to net sales decreased by 2.8 per cent and that of gross margin increased by a like amount. The trends are, obviously, favourable.

POWERPACK INDIA LIMITED
Ratios of Cost of Goods Sold and Gross Margin to Net Sales

Year ended March 31	Net Sales Rs Lakhs	Cost of Goods Rs Lakhs	Gross Margin Rs Lakhs	Ratio to Net Sales of	
				Cost of Goods sold %	Gross Margin %
A	3513	2662	851	75.8	24.2
B	4277	3466	811	81.0	19.0
C	4779	3691	1088	77.2	22.8
D	5423	4092	1331	75.5	24.5
E	5690	4183	1507	73.5	26.5
F	6145	4484	1661	73.0	27.0

Ratio of Operating Expenses to Net Sales

Operating expenses comprise administrative and general expenses which are directly related to the normal operations of a company but do not form part of cost of goods sold. A study of the year-to-year change in the relationship of operating expenses to net sales is important because it reveals the ability of the management to adjust expenses to changing trading conditions.

The three elements of operating expenses, namely, selling expenses, administrative expenses, and general expenses, should preferably be shown separately on the profit and loss account but almost invariably are not. A number of selling expenses such as advertising and sales promotional expenses, delivery expenses, and salesmen's salaries, commission and travelling expenses, usually vary with the volume of sales. Administrative and general expenses tend to remain approximately the same unless the sales activity is considerably expanded.

The ratio of net sales to each type of operating expense (selling, administrative, and general) shows the percentage of the net sales revenue that has been consumed by each class of expenses. The percentages also facilitate inter-firm comparison of companies operating within the same industry or line of business.

Exhibit 28 shows that, as compared with the increase of 75 per cent in net sales of Powerpack India Ltd. during the six-year period, ended March 31, Year A through Year F, inclusive, operating expenses increased by 86 per cent but the increase mostly came during Year F and consumed a larger portion of the net sales realisation than the average of the preceding five years as will be seen from the following table:

POWERPACK INDIA LIMITED
Ratios of Operating Expenses and Operating Income to Net Sales

Year ended March 31	Net Sales Rs Lakhs	Operating Expenses Rs Lakhs	Operating Income Rs Lakhs	Ratio to Net Sales	
				Operating Expenses %	Operating Income %
A	3513	182	669	5.2	19.0
B	4277	202	609	4.7	14.3
C	4779	237	851	5.0	17.8
D	5423	267	1064	4.9	19.6
F	5690	290	1217	5.1	21.4
F	6145	338	1323	5.5	21.5

Ratio of Operating Income to Net Sales

Operating income represents the difference between gross margin on sales and operating expenses, and is exclusive of non-operating income and expenses, interest, income tax, and extraordinary gains and losses. It is one of the most important figures in the profit and loss account which reveals the profitableness of sales, that is, of the regular buying, manufacturing, and selling operations of a business.

It varies with changes in sales, cost of goods sold, and operating expenses, and should be related to sales by computing the ratio of operating income to net sales, as shown in the last column of the table above, to show the number of paise that remain after cost of goods sold and operating expenses are deducted from the sales rupee.

In the case of Powerpack India Ltd. the ratio of operating income to net sales increased rapidly from Year B to Year E because both the cost of goods sold and operating expenses increased at a comparatively slower rate than did net sales. During Year F, net sales increased by about eight per cent over the previous year but operating expenses rose by some 17 per cent. While cost of goods sold increased in line with net sales in absolute rupee amounts, operating income in Year F was larger at Rs 1,323 lakh compared with Rs 1,217 lakh in Year E, but the ratio of operating income to net sales remained almost unchanged.

Operating Ratio

The "operating ratio" which is the percentage of net sales absorbed jointly by cost of goods sold and operating expenses is obtained by deducting the ratio of operating income to net sales from 100 per cent or by dividing the total of cost of goods sold and operating expenses by net sales and expressing the result as a percentage. Thus, using the sales and cost data of Powerpack India Ltd. for Year F

$$\frac{\text{Total Cost and Expenses : Rs 4,822 lakh}}{\text{Net Sales : Rs 6,145 lakh}} = \text{Operating Ratio : 78.5\%}$$

The same figure, quite logically, can be obtained by deducting from 100 per cent the ratio of operating income to net sales for Year F which, as shown in the table at page 184 was 21.5 per cent. The higher the operating ratio the less favourable the situation naturally is since the resulting smaller amount of operating income may not be sufficient to meet interest and dividend payment requirements and other corporate needs. Companies with low operating ratios and consequently high ratios of operating income to net sales, therefore, have less to worry about in periods of business slackness because their profits can shrink considerably before the danger level is reached.

The operating ratios for Powerpack India Ltd. for each of the years, ended March 31, A through F, are shown in the table below:

POWERPACK INDIA LIMITED

Operating Ratios and Trend Percentages in Net Sales and Costs and Expenses

Year ended March 31	Net Sales Rs Lakhs	Costs and Expenses Rs Lakhs	Operating Ratio	Trend Percentages	
				Net Sales	Costs and Expenses
A	3513	2844	81.0	100	100
B	4277	3668	85.8	122	129
C	4779	3928	82.2	136	138
D	5423	4359	80.4	154	153
E	5690	4473	78.6	162	157
F	6145	4822	78.5	175	170

It will be noted that, after rising to 85.8 per cent in Year B from 81 per cent in Year A, the operating ratio tended to decline steadily and came to 78.5 per cent in Year F. This was because, between Year B and Year F, net sales increased by 44 per cent, or Rs 1,868 lakh, but cost and expenses increased by Rs 154 lakh or 31 per cent since the company could spread its manufacturing expenses over a larger production.

Ratio of Net Profit to Net Sales

Net profit is that portion of the total income (net sales plus non-operating income and gains) which remains for the owners or shareholders after all costs, expenses and charges, including interest and income tax have been met. Since it is out of this amount that dividends and other distributions and allocations are made, the larger it is the larger, in theory at any rate, can the appropriations be.

The ratio of net profit to net sales is of utmost importance, therefore, to the shareholders. It is worked out simply by dividing the amount of net profit by the amount of net sales and expressing the quotient as a percentage as shown in the table below:

POWERPACK INDIA LIMITED

Ratio of Net Profit to Net Sales

Year ended March 31	Net Profit Rs Lakhs	Net Sales Rs Lakhs	Ratio %	Trend Percentages	
				Net Profit	Net Sales
A	223	3513	6.3	100	100
B	253	4277	5.9	113	122
C	348	4779	7.3	156	136
D	475	5423	8.8	213	154
E	496	5690	8.7	222	162
F	536	6145	8.7	240	175

Ratio of Net Sales to Operating Assets

The ratio of operating income to net sales should be studied in conjunction with the ratio of operating income to operating assets employed in obtaining the sales volume. This latter ratio provides a measure of the profitable use of operating assets employed in the business.

At times, the amount of operating income may be satisfactory in relation to net sales, but may be insufficient in relation to total operating assets because the volume of sales may be low in relation to the plant capacity, that is, the amount of capital invested in the fixed assets used in obtaining the sales volume.

The ratio of net sales to total operating assets, which is usually referred to as the "turnover of operating assets", is computed by dividing net sales by total operating assets, that is the depreciated value of fixed assets. It provides a measure of the use that is being made of the assets employed for productive purposes. Thus

$$\frac{\text{Net Sales : Rs 3,994 lakh}}{\text{Net Operating Assets : Rs 7,381 lakh}} = 54.1\%$$

POWERPACK INDIA LIMITED

Ratios of Net Sales and Operating Income to Operating Assets

Year ended May 31	Net Sales Rs Lakhs	Operating Income Rs Lakhs	Operating Assets Rs Lakhs	Ratio to Operating Assets of	
				Net Sales Times	Operating Income %
A	3513	669	295	11.9	226.8
B	4277	609	417	10.3	146.0
C	4779	851	642	7.4	132.6
D	5423	1064	859	6.3	123.9
E	5690	1217	944	6.0	128.9
F	6145	1323	945	6.5	140.0

Ratio of Operating Income to Operating Assets

This complimentary ratio measures the earnings potential of a business and is obtained by dividing operating income by the depreciated value of fixed assets.

It will be noted from the table above providing the ratios of net sales and operating income to net operating assets of Powerpack India Ltd. for the six years, ended March 31, A through F, that the company had been "turning over" its net fixed assets very fast and earning a very high rate of return on the capital invested in fixed productive assets.

Although with the establishment of a new factory, the turnover figure declined perceptibly after Year B, it still averaged 6.5 times indicating that through its annual sales volume the company was recovering several times the capital invested in productive assets. It was not particularly susceptible, therefore, to adverse market trends or disruption of production owing to labour trouble.

The table also indicates that the company was earning a very high rate of return on the invested capital. Although the income tended to decline in the three years B, C and D, it began to rise thereafter because of the improvement in the gross margin on sales and the absorption of almost the same percentage of net sales by operating expenses.

Break-even Point

The costs and expenses of a business are generally of two types. Some increase or decrease in line with the sales volume. These are designated variable expenses and include the cost of goods sold (excluding depreciation) and direct selling expenses. There are certain expenses, however, which do not so vary with the sales volume. These are called fixed expenses and comprise administrative and general expenses, interest charges and, to some extent, depreciation. They remain fixed so long as the sales volume does not exceed a certain level. Once a new level of sales is reached a larger amount of sales expenses may remain fixed till the next expansion in sales takes place.

When the net sales of a company are just the total of fixed and variable expenses, there will be neither a net profit nor a net loss. In other words, the company will "break-even" at that "point" of net sales. If net sales were to rise above this point, the variable expenses would increase, no doubt, but fixed expense would not and, consequently, would absorb a lower percentage of the increased net sales income. There would be left a profit, therefore, which would continue to rise as the sales volume tended to increase.

If net sales were to fall below the break-even point, the variable expenses would, of course, decrease but fixed expenses would stay at their previous level and claim a larger percentage than before of the decreased sales value. A loss would result and would tend to increase if net sales declined further.

The break-even point can be determined by preparing a graph or it may be computed mathematically. In either case it is necessary to have available the sales and expense data for a number of years or accounting periods and also to divide the expenses into fixed costs and variable costs. In preparing the graph, the sales volume is usually measured along the horizontal axis and costs and expenses along the vertical axis. Lines or curves are drawn to pass through the different points on the graph and the break-even point is located where the total cost and sales lines or curves intersect.

It is to be emphasised that a break-even point chart is valid only for a relatively narrow range of production and sales at a given time. As production and sales increase beyond this range, some of the fixed costs also must increase, and at a point below this range, some fixed costs may be reduced and some variable costs may not decline in full proportion. Only within a reasonable range will the relationships hold true.

The break-even point is usually determined by using historical accounting data, but estimated or budgeted figures can be used to arrive at decisions concerning sales prices, sales mix, product quality, expansion of capacity, and management improvements. For example, if a company has planned an expansion which will increase its fixed costs by a certain amount, a break-even point analysis will indicate the level of sales volume that must be reached for the company to break-even and fully recover the projected fixed costs.

The data necessary for the determination of the break-even point is usually available only to the internal analyst especially where detailed cost records are maintained. As such, break-even point analysis is essentially a management tool which can be used in forecasting the probable unit cost at varying levels of production, or the sales volume necessary to justify a plant expansion, in evaluating management performance by comparing and evaluating actual break-even results with budgeted or predetermined levels and in making decisions regarding company policies concerning expansion and future goods. The external analyst normally does not have access to data exact enough to draw reliable conclusions. When the sales volume is varying substantially, nevertheless, he may be able to arrive at approximate yet meaningful conclusions by making use of the published data for the past number of years.

CHAPTER 24

The Cash-flow Statement

The methods of financial statement analysis discussed so far are indeed helpful in their own way in locating the points of strength and weakness in the current and long-term financial condition of a business enterprise. They also enable an external analyst to study the change, that may have taken place over the years in the firm's financial status and to assess whether these have been favourable or unfavourable.

The methods do not prove of much help to the analyst, however to find answers to the questions that often arise in the mind of those not having knowledge of book-keeping and accountancy or to explain the situations such people find puzzling. It happens, for instance, that the results of operations of a business show an attractive profit on balance but the directors are unable to declare and pay a generous dividend because sufficient cash is not available to make the distribution.

In yet another common situation, a firm appears to be in a comfortable position financially and is operating profitably year after year, but may be unable to meet maturing obligations without taking recourse to long-term borrowing or raising additional share capital. Shareholders and creditors wish to be explained in such a situation, what has happened to the cash profits generated.

To provide answers to these and similar questions, it is customary to prepare special types of statements designed to throw light on the movement of funds into and out of a business or within the sphere of activity of the business. These statements are, of course, complementary to, and not independent of, the balance sheet and the profit and loss account but are capable of providing information which cannot be easily obtained or obtained at all, from the two principal statements.

Types of Statements

Using the details provided by the balance sheet and the profit and loss account and the numerous annexures, schedules, and notes appended thereto, four types of statements can be prepared to answer specific queries or to explain particular situations. These are:

1. *The Cash-flow Statement* which is designed to throw light on the movement of cash funds into and out of a business and answer questions sought to be replied to by shareholders, investors, and trade creditors.

2. *Statements of Change in Net Working Capital* showing the increase or decrease in net working capital that may have taken place between two balance sheet dates and listing the causes for the changes as either sources or applications of working capital funds.
3. *The Statement Accounting for Variations in the Tangible Net Worth,* or Owners' Equity is a simpler report for a lay reader to understand than any of the other three reports.
4. *The Funds Statement or Statement of Sources and Applications of Funds* which, in fact, is a condensed report on how the activities of the firm have been financed and how the financial resources at the disposal of the firm have been utilised during the period to which the report is related.

Cash-flow Statement

The purpose of preparing a cash-flow statement as mentioned above, is to find out how much cash resources moved into the business and how much of them moved out during a particular accounting period. It supplements the funds statements and shows the causes or reasons for the increase or decrease during the period in the cash balance shown on the balance sheet.

The profit and loss account though giving details of the income and expenditure during the accounting period, proves of little help for the reason that the amount of surplus or deficit shown therein hardly ever equals the amount by which the cash balance is reported on the balance sheet as having increased or decreased.

There is always a difference which is caused by several original adjustment and transfer journal entries passed at the time of finalisation of the annual accounts. Under the almost universally followed double-entry book-keeping system, financial transactions are recorded on an accrual rather than on a cash basis. This necessitates passing of adjustment and other entries to transfer the amounts of income and expenses not relating to the year's operations and to list them under appropriate heads on the balance sheet.

Non-cash Transactions

Such transfer entries represent what are called non-cash transactions which are neither sources nor applications of cash resources. Included among these are:

1. Income accrued but not received yet taken credit for in the profit and loss account.
2. Expenses accrued but not paid for yet included among items of expenditure.

3. Adjustments relating to prior years' income and expenditure.
4. Write-offs of unrecoverable debts and dues.
5. Increases or decreases in the book-value of non-current assets.
6. Provisions for bad debts, advances, and deposits.
7. Provisions for depreciation, depletion and amortisation.
8. Profit or loss on sale of investments and fixed assets.
9. Appropriation of the profit subject to tax.

Even though the above and other similar transactions do not involve the receipt or payment of cash, they do affect the final profit or loss shown on the profit and loss account and usually put it at variance with the increase or decrease in the cash shown on the balance sheet. To reconcile the difference, it is necessary to eliminate the effect on the reported profit or loss of the non-cash transactions by reversing the entries which originally introduced them. In other words, what is required to be done is to effect adjustments of the reported profit and loss account items with a view to restating them on a cash basis.

Preparing a Cash-flow Statement

An internal analyst can readily prepare a cash-flow statement by referring to his company's cash book, expenses ledger and the original transfer and journal entries passed at the time of the annual finalisation of accounts. But, the exercise usually proves laborious and time consuming and the analyst would do well to prefer the alternative approach which is less demanding in both effort and time.

This requires the use of the balance sheet and the profit and loss account for the year, and a list of non-cash transactions recorded during the year. The procedure usually followed in the preparation of a cash-flow statement adopting this approach is briefly as follows:

1. A comparative balance sheet is prepared to show increases and decreases in items of assets, liabilities, and owners' equity or net worth.
2. A work sheet is then prepared having debit and credit columns for recording net changes and similar columns for recording adjustments eliminating non-cash transactions.
3. In the debit column under "net changes" are entered increases in assets, decreases in liabilities and owners' equity all of which represent uses of cash.
4. In the credit column under "net changes" are mentioned increases in liabilities and owners' equity, and decreases in assets all of which indicate sources of cash.
5. Expense items from the profit and loss account are entered in the debit column and revenue items in the credit column in detail and

not just the net changes in these items. Increase in inventory of finished goods and work-in-progress is posted in the credit column after net sales and the decrease in the inventory is entered in the debit column ahead of the expense items.

6. Thus, while filling up the work sheet, net changes only in the balance sheet items are entered, income and expense items are posted directly from the profit and loss account.

7. Using the additional information available, adjustment entries are recorded against concerned items to remove the effect, if any, of original adjustment and journal entries not involving either a source or an application of cash.

8. After the adjustments required have been entered, net changes in several balance sheet items will have been eliminated on being transferred to concerned items from the profit and loss account.

9. The remaining of the balance sheet changes and items from profit and loss account representing cash transactions are then used to prepare the cash-flow statement.

10. If cash has increased during the period, sources increasing cash are listed first, but the order is reversed if there is decrease in cash. In this situation, uses of cash are listed first and sources thereafter so that the net decrease in cash can be readily worked out.

Some Guidelines

For a person having no formal knowledge of bookkeeping and accountancy, preparing a cash-flow statement using published financial information usually proves more formidable an undertaking than preparing the other types of statements. Not having undergone training as an accountant, he usually has no comprehension of either the purpose of the original adjustment and transfer journal entries passed, or their impact on the cash balance. The following guide-lines are being provided, therefore, to help him carry out the required adjustments on the work sheet and prepare the final cash-flow statement therefrom.

1. Sundry Debtors

An increase in Sundry Debtors shows the amount of current sales not received in cash. A decrease, on the other hand, indicates receipt of cash against sales effected in the past. On the work sheet, an increase is to be shown as a credit to Sundry Debtors and, simultaneously, as a debit to Net Sales to show the amount of cash actually received during the year through sales. Conversely, a decrease is entered on the work sheet as a debit to Sundry Debtors and a credit to Net Sales to record the additional amount of cash received from sales, past and present.

2. Provision for Bad Debts

On published balance sheets, Sundry Debtors are reported "net", that is, after deduction of the provision for Bad and Doubtful Debts. While entering the amounts on the work sheet, Sundry Debtors should be entered "gross" among the assets and the provision for Bad Debts among the liabilities. Net increase in the provision is to be debited to Net Sales while net decrease is to be credited to cancel the effect of the original transfer entry which is non-cash in nature.

3. Inventories

On the balance sheet, inventories represent the cost of manufacture of finished goods and the expenditure incurred on the work-in-progress till the date of the balance sheet. On the profit and loss account the opening balance of inventories is recorded on the expenditure side and the closing or year-end balance on the income or revenue side. Alternatively, net increase in inventory is added to the revenue while net decrease is deducted.

If the comparative balance sheet shows a net increase in Inventories, on the work sheet it is to be entered as credited to Inventories in the balance sheet part and debit to Increase in Inventories in the profit and loss account section. In the case of a decrease in Inventories, it is to be debited to Inventories on the work sheet and credited to Increase in Inventories.

4. Accrued Income

This item on the balance sheet shows the amount of rent, interest, dividends and similar income due but not received during the year. This is a non-cash transaction and the entry has to be reversed to eliminate its effect on the final profit or loss. An increase is to be transferred to the debit of Other Income on the work sheet to show that the revenue was not collected in cash. A decrease is to be transferred to the credit of Other Income to show the additional revenue received in cash.

5. Loans and Advances

All transactions recorded under the head are in cash and hence no adjustments need be recorded on the work sheet. A decrease is a source of cash while an increase is an application of cash.

6. Non-current Assets

All transactions being in cash no adjustments are needed. An increase in the year-end balance is an application of cash and a decrease is a source of cash.

7. Fixed Assets at Cost

An increase in Fixed Assets at Cost indicates the application of cash for purchase of fixed assets. The figure appearing on the comparative balance sheet, however, does not indicate the total amount of cash used since it is arrived at after deducting from the year-end figure of Fixed Assets at Cost, the book-value of assets scrapped and/or sold. The deduction is an original adjustment entry not involving use of cash and needs to be reversed. This is done by debiting to Fixed Asset at Cost, the book-value of assets scrapped and/or sold and crediting it to Profit/Loss on Sale of Assets (see Item 15).

8. Depreciation

It is customary to show Accumulated Depreciation on the balance sheet, as a deduction from the amount of Fixed Assets at Cost. The annual depreciation charge does not involve use of cash and is an original transfer entry to be reversed while preparing a cash-flow statement. But, as in the case of Fixed Assets at Cost, the increase in Accumulated Depreciation stated on the comparative balance sheet is a "net" figure arrived at by deducting from the amount of depreciation charged to the profit and loss account for the year, the write-back depreciation of fixed assets scrapped and/or sold. To effect the adjustment, the amount of depreciation written-back is credited to Accumulated Depreciation and debited to Profit/Loss on Sale of Assets. (see Item 15 below).

9. Sundry Creditors

A decrease in Sundry Creditors is to be transferred to the debit of Materials Consumed on the profit and loss account to show the amount of cash paid during the year for purchases made in the past but not paid for. Similarly, an increase in Sundry Creditors is to be transferred to the credit of Materials Consumed.

10. Accrued Expenses

An increase in Accrued Expenses (Salaries, Wages, Rent, Rates, Taxes, Interest, etc.) is to be transferred to the credit of the respective accounts to show that the amounts were not paid in cash. This adjustment will restate on cash basis the expenses recorded on the profit and loss account.

11. Non-current Liabilities

An increase in non-current liabilities, such as term-loans, is a source of cash while a decrease is an application of cash. As in the case of non-current assets, no adjustments are needed and the figures on the work sheet can be transferred to the Cash-flow Statement.

12. Provision for Taxation

Every company and firm is required to pay income tax on the profit earned. The payment is to be made, however, only when a demand is made by the Income Tax Department. To meet this contingency, the normal practice is to set aside a part of the profit as a Provision for Taxation. When payment is made, it is debited to the provision and any balance remaining is carried forward to the next year. A decrease is added to the Provision for Taxation while an increase is deducted to show the amount of cash paid to meet the liability. The procedure of adjustment is shown by the following analysis:

	Rs'000
Provision for Taxation : Opening Balance	5,066
Add:Transferred from Profit and Loss Account	63.273
	68,339
Deduct : Closing Balance	3.949
Cash paid during the year	64.390

The same result will be obtained if the comparative balance is used.

	Rs'000
Provision for Taxation as per Profit and Loss Account	63,273
Add: Net Decrease in Provision	1.117
Cash used for payment of Income Tax	64.390

13. Provision for Dividend

An increase is to be debited and a decrease is to be credited to the Provision for Dividend to get the amount of cash used to pay dividend. Thus:

	Rs'000
Provision for Dividend: Opening Balance	10,151
Add: Amount Transferred from Profit and Loss Account	11.279
	21,430
Deduct: Closing Balance	11.279
Cash used to pay Dividend	10.151

Contd…

	Rs'000
Alternatively,	
Amount transferred from	
Profit and Loss Account	11,279
Deduct: Increase in Provision	1,128
Cash used to pay Dividend	10,151

14. Owners' Equity

An increase in Net Worth because of a fresh issue of share capital is a cash transaction and does not call for an adjustment on the work sheet. Similarly, a decrease in Owners' Equity brought about by redemption of preference shares is a cash transaction and no adjustment is again necessary. The increase in Reserves owing to transfer of surplus from the profit and loss account is a non-cash transaction, however, and the adjustment entry needs to be reversed. To effect the adjustment on the work sheet, debit Owners' Equity with the amount of surplus originally transferred and credit Retained Surplus.

15. Profit/Loss on Sale of Assets

On published profit and loss accounts, the profit earned on sale of an asset is included in Other Income while the loss sustained is included in Other Expenses. In preparing a cash-flow statement, it is advisable to show these entries separately because they are of an exceptional nature unlike regular receivables like rent, licence fees, consultation charges, interest and dividends.

Published financial statements provide the cost of purchase of the different assets but hardly ever the amount received on the sale of any of them. Invariably, only the profit or loss made on the deal is indicated. Using the supplementary data supplied and carrying out the adjustment indicated in Items 7 and 8 above, the amount of cash received can be worked out as under, provided the profit and loss on sale of assets has not been subjected to adjustments the details of which are not disclosed.

An asset purchased at Rs 16,68,845 of which Rs 16,13,115 have been written off as depreciation in earlier years account is now sold at a profit of Rs 28,815. The amount of cash received on the sale can be arrived at by writing the ledger account as follows:

Sale of Assets Account

	Rs		Rs
To Fixed Asset		By Accumulated	
at cost	16,68,845	Depreciation	16,13,115
To Profit and Loss Account	28,815	By Cash	84,545
	16,97,660		16,97,660

In other words what is to be done is to find out the depreciated value of the assets, add to it the profit made (or deduct the loss sustained) and get the amount of cash received. Thus:

	Rs
Original Cost of the Asset	16,68,845
Deduct: Depreciation written off	16,13,115
Depreciated Value	55,730
Add: Profit made on Sale	28,815
Cash Received on Sale	84,545

CHAPTER 25

Statement of Changes in Net Working Capital

More comprehensive than the Cash-flow Statement but less broad in its extent and purpose than the Funds Statement, is the Statement of Changes in Net Working Capital. The Cash-flow Statement, as already explained, exhibits how cash moved during an accounting period into and out of a business stating the sources from which the cash was obtained, or was received, and the applications or uses to which it was put.

The Statement of Changes in Net Working Capital takes a broader view and analyses the changes, that is, increases or decreases, that may have taken place in individual current assets and current liabilities and the net working capital in general. Such changes, it will be realised, whether taking place during a single or over a period of years, are of interest to the owners and managers of the business as well as to its short-term creditors.

To the owners and the management, they reveal the success or otherwise of the deliberate policy put into effect to strengthen the financial base of the company and whether an adequate amount of working funds would be available in the future to support an expanding volume of sales. To current or short-term creditors, the changes indicate the extent to which the firm is dependent on outside finance to carry out its normal operations and the margin of safety available to those having financial dealings with it.

It does not serve adequately the purpose of analysis, however, to only compute the increases and decreases that have taken place in individual current items of assets and liabilities. It is equally important to find out the reasons and the factors responsible for these changes. Factors bringing about increases in the net working capital are designated as sources of additional working capital while those responsible for a decrease in the net working capital are captioned as applications or uses of working funds additionally introduced.

A statement of changes in net working capital may be defined, therefore, as a schedule which shows the changes that have taken place during an accounting period in the net working capital employed in a business and goes on to list each of these changes as either a source or an application of the short-term funds deployed.

Sources and Applications

The common sources increasing net working capital include:

1. Profit earned from current operations, inclusive of the provision for depreciations, depletion and amortisation of fixed, wasting, and intangible assets respectively
2. Profit earned on sale of fixed or non-current assets
3. Profit earned on sale of temporary investment
4. Refund of income tax and other non-operating receipts
5. Short-term loans from banks, owners, directors, employees, and the public
6. Trade creditors
7. Issue of debenture bonds or raising of long-term loans from institutions
8. Raising of additional share-capital.

The major applications or uses of net working capital include:

1. Payment of dividends or performance and equity shares.
2. Writing off of operating and extraordinary losses
3. Redeeming preference shares and debentures
4. Repayment of long-term loans
5. Purchases of additional fixed assets, intangible assets or long-term investments
6. Replacement of fixed assets.

Form of Statement

The changes taking place in the net working capital of a business enterprise between two balance sheet dates can be analysed and presented in the form of a statement which is usually made up of two parts. The first or upper part lists the increases or decreases in rupee amounts in individual items of current assets and current liabilities as also in net working capital. The second or lower part indicates the sources from which working funds have been obtained and the different applications to which they have been put. In other words it provides the reason for the increase or decrease in net working capital.

A statement showing the changes in net working capital that have taken place in a single accounting year is prepared by making use of the balance sheet and the profit and loss account for that year and the supplementary information made available by notes, schedules and annexures appended thereto.

If it is desired to prepare a statement of changes in net working capital over a period of years, it is essential to have and to analyse the balance sheet and the profit and loss account for each of the years included in the time period to get a complete picture. The statement may be prepared in greater or lesser detail depending upon the requirements of the analyst and the information supplied by the basic financial statements.

Statement of Changes in Net Working Capital — Illustrations

Fairmaid Corporation (India) Limited

The statement of changes in the net working capital of Fairmaid Corporation (India) Ltd., manufacturers of cosmetics and beauty products, shown in Exhibit 30 has been prepared by using the company's balance sheet and profit and loss account for the current year ended March 31, which also provides corresponding figures for the immediately preceding year, and the following supplementary information furnished by attached annexures, schedules and notes.

1. The book-value of fixed assets increased during the year by Rs 17,85,448 as follows:

Assets	Additions/ Transfers Rs	Deductions/ Transfers Rs
Plant and Machinery	23,09,964	8,37,621
Furniture and Equipment	4,22,067	2,10,909
Automobiles and Trucks	2,04,720	1,02,733
	29,36,751	11,51,263
Net Increase	—	17,85,488
	29,36,751	29,36,751

2. Depreciation charged to the profit and loss account of the year was Rs 30,18,517 while Rs 9,52,780 were written back as accumulated depreciation on fixed assets, other than buildings, sold, scrapped or transferred during the year. The net increase in depreciation of buildings, plant, machinery and other equipment provided till March 31 of the current year was, therefore, Rs 20,65,737.
3. Book-value of capital work-in-progress and advances against orders placed, increased by Rs 3,32,212.
4. The net increase in the book-value of fixed assets during the year was thus Rs 51,963.
5. The profit from operations during the year after providing for depreciation of fixed assets was Rs 17,17,69,485. To this was added Rs 75,23,274 as prior years adjustments and from the total was deducted Rs 13,03,400 as loss on sale of investment while Rs 13,14,00,000 were provided for taxation of current profits.

6. After making these adjustments, the net profit for the year was reported as Rs 4,65,89,359.
7. Two interim dividends together claiming Rs 2,41,69,500 were paid out of the profit for the year and a final dividend expected to absorb Rs 33,40,500 was proposed for payment after the annual general meeting to be held on July 30.

Using the company's balance sheet as at March 31 of the current year, and the supplementary information given above, a statement of changes in net working capital during the year under review can be prepared in three stages as detailed below.

Method of Preparation

The first stage in the process is to prepare a comparative balance sheet of the company as at March 31 listing the individual items of assets, liabilities and net worth and showing the increases and decreases that have taken place during the year. This appears as Exhibit 29.

The second stage in the construction of the statement is to prepare an intermediate statement (Exhibit 30) listing only the items of current assets and current liabilities and arriving at the figure of net working capital for the current year and the immediately preceding year.

The statement should show the increases or decreases in individual items of current assets and current liabilities as also in the net working capital that have taken place during the current year. According to the Intermediate Statement (Exhibit 30), net working capital of Fairmaid Corporation (India) Ltd. increased during the year by Rs 1,37,28,000 following a net increase of Rs 25,28,000 in total current assets and a much larger net decrease of Rs 1,12,00,000 in total current liabilities.

The third stage in the process is to prepare an abridged statement of changes in net working capital by bringing into the picture the non-current items of assets, liabilities, and net worth shown in the comparative balance sheet (Exhibit 29). The purpose of introducing the statement is to classify and analyse the reasons for the total change (increase or decrease) in net working capital. In other words the purpose of the abridged statement is to indicate the various sources from which additional working funds were obtained and the various uses or applications these were put to.

FAIRMAID CORPORATION (INDIA) LIMITED

**Abridged Statement of Changes in Net Working Capital
during the Current Year ended March 31, 20__**

		Rs in Thousands
Sources increasing Net Working Capital:		
Increase in Net worth	19,080	
Increase in Accumulated Depreciation	2,066	
Total Sources		21,146
Applications decreasing Net Working Capital		
Acquisition of Fixed Assets — Net	1,785	
Addition to Capital Work-in-progress	333	
Addition to Tax Deposit	5,300	
Total Applications		7,418
Increase in Net Working Capital		13,728

The sources increasing net working capital are three, namely,

1. Decrease in non-current assets, their conversion into cash or current assets
2. Increase in non-current liabilities as through an issuance of debenture bonds or raising of long term loans
3. Increase in net worth through an issue of fresh capital and plough-back of operating and non-operating profits.

The uses or applications decreasing net-working capital are also three in number and are:

1. Increase in non-current assets, such as fixed assets purchased by reducing cash
2. Decrease in non-current liabilities, such as redemption of debenture bonds or repayment of long-term loans by reducing cash
3. Decrease in net worth as takes place when preference shares are redeemed or when an operating loss is sustained.

It will be noted that the increase during the year under review in the amount of accumulated depreciation has been treated as a source increasing net working capital. The reason, as explained earlier, is that although shown as an item of operating cost in the profit and loss account, the annual depreciation charge is not an expense to meet which cash has to be paid or a cheque has to be drawn.

Not affecting the amount of cash on hand or in bank (a current asset) depreciation constitutes neither a source nor an application of net working capital. But, treating depreciation as an item of expenditure reduces the operations profit for the year which is one of the sources of net working capital. So to determine the amount of working capital provided additionally by current operations it

Exhibit 29

FAIRMAID CORPORATION LIMITED
Comparative Balance Sheet as at March 31, 20___

(Rs in Thousands)

Items	Previous Year	Current Year	Changes during the year	
			Increases	Decreases
ASSETS				
Current Assets				
Cash	22,635	12,741		9,894
Sundry Debtors – Net	10,907	15,373	4,466	
Inventories	109,582	113,795	4,213	
Accruals	30	-		30
Advance and Deposits	8,217	11,990	3,773	
Total Current Assets	151,371	153,899	12,452	9,924
	======	======	======	======
Miscellaneous Assets	2,400	7,700	5,300	
	======	======	======	
Fixed Assets – Gross	40,032	41,817	1,785	
Less: Depreciation	14,938	17,004	2,066	
Fixed Assets – Net	25,094	24,813		281
Addition: Capital Work-in-Progress	1,464	1,797	333	
Total Fixed Assets – Net	26,558	26,610	333	281
	======	======	======	======
TOTAL ASSETS	180,329	188,209	18,085	10,205
	======	======	======	======

Contd...

Exhibit 29 (Contd...)

FAIRMAID CORPORATION LIMITED
Comparative Balance Sheet as at March 31, 20___

(Rs in Thousands)

Items	Previous Year	Current Year	Changes during the year	
			Increases	Decreases
LIABILITIES AND NET WORTH				
Current Liabilities				
Sundry Creditors and Acceptances	49,535	34,071		15,464
Advances and Deposits	495	823	328	
Unclaimed Dividends	4,221	3,717		504
Short Term Loans	42	42	-	-
Provisions	27,675	32,115	4,440	
Total Current Liabilities	81,968	70,768	4,768	15,968
Net Worth				
Share Capital	39,300	39,300		
Reserves and Surplus	59,061	78,141	19,080	
Total Net Worth	98,361	117,441	19,080	
TOTAL LIABILITIES AND NET WORTH	180,329	188,209	23,848	15,968

Exhibit 30

FAIRMAID CORPORATION (INDIA) LIMITED
Schedule of Net Working Items

(Rupees in Thousands)

Items	March 31 Previous	March 31 Current	Changes during the Year Increases	Changes during the Year Decreases
Current Assets				
Cash	22,635	12,741		9,894
Sundry Debtors – Net	10,907	15,373	4,466	
Inventories	109,582	113,795	4,213	
Accruals	30	-		30
Advances & Deposits	8,217	11,990	3,773	
TOTAL CURRENT ASSETS	151,371	153,899	12,452	9,924
Current Liabilities				
Sundry Creditors & Acceptances	49,535	34,071		15,464
Advances & Deposits	495	823	328	
Unclaimed Dividends	4,221	3,717		504
Short-term Loans	42	42	-	
Provisions	27,675	32,115	4,440	
TOTAL CURRENT LIABILITIES	81,968	70,768	4,768	15,968
Net Working Capital	69,403	83,131		6,044
Increase in Net Working Capital			7,684	13,728
			7,684	7,684

becomes necessary to eliminate the effect of depreciation adjustment entries.

This may be done in two ways. If only the balance sheet is being made use of in casting the statement of changes in net working capital, the accretion during the year to the amount of depreciation written off fixed assets to-date, should be treated as a source increasing net working capital. But, if use is being made of the profit and loss account also, the profit before providing for depreciation should be treated as a source of working capital and not the reported operating profit.

The fourth and final stage is the preparation of a statement of changes in net working capital is to make use of the data provided by the comparative balance sheet, the additional information furnished by the profit and loss account and the details contained in the notes, annexures and schedules appended to the basic financial statements. The final statement of changes in net working capital of Fairmaid Corporation (India) Ltd. during the current year ended March 31, is presented is Exhibit 31.

Exhibit 31

FAIRMAID CORPORATION (INDIA) LTD.

Statement of Changes in Net Working Capital during Current Year, Ended March 31, 20__

Rs in Thousands

Sources: Increasing Net Working Capital		
Profit from Current operations subject		
to Tax and Adjustments	171,769	
Add : Provision for Depreciation	3,019	1,74,788
Refund of Excise duty, sales tax and		
adjustments in respect of prior years		7,523
Total Sources		1,82,311
Applications : Decreasing Net Working Capital		
Acquisition of Fixed Assets — Net	1,785	
Investment in Capital work-in-progress	333	
Depreciation written back	952	3,070
Loss on investment written off		1,303
Additional Deposit under the Companies		
Deposit (Surcharge on Income tax) Scheme		5,300
Provision for Income Tax		1,31,400
Dividends : paid and proposed		27,510
Total Applications		1,68,583
		=======
Increase in Net Working Capital during the Year		13,728

Statement of Variations in Net Worth or Owners' Equity

The need for making adjustments for items consisting neither a source nor an application of net working capital such as depreciation, renders the statement of changes in net working capital somewhat puzzling to a person not having adequate training in or knowledge of, accountancy. For him a somewhat simpler statement to understand is the one accounting for variations in owner's equity or net worth.

Exhibit 32

FAIRMAID CORPORATION (INDIA) LIMITED

Statement Accounting for Variations in Owner's Equity during Current Year Ended March 31, 20___

		Rs in Thousands
Net Increase in Owner's Equity		
Owner's Equity as on March 31, current year	1,17,441	
Owner's Equity as on March 31, previous year	98,361	
Net Increase in Owners' Equity		19,080
Increase in Owner's Equity accounted for by—		
Increase in Assets :		
Sundry Creditors	4,466	
Inventories	4,213	
Advances and Deposits	3,773	
Miscellaneous Assets	5,300	
Fixed Assets – Net	333	18,085
Decrease in Liabilities:		
Sundry Creditors and Acceptances	15,464	
Unclaimed Dividends	504	15,968
Total Increase in Owner's Equity		34,053
Decrease in Owner's Equity accounted for by—		
Decrease in Assets:		
Cash	9,894	
Accruals	30	
Fixed Assets — Net	281	10,205
Increase in Liabilities:		
Advances and Deposits	328	
Provisions	4,440	4,768
Total Decrease in Owner's Equity		14,973
Total Increase in Owner's Equity	34,053	
Less : Total Decrease in Owner's Equity	14,973	
Net Increase in Owner's Equity		19,080

Such a statement can be prepared simply by rearranging the information provided by the comparative balance sheet without taking into consideration items requiring an adjustment. If, however, it is desired to prepare a more elaborate statement, recourse can be had to the information supplied by the profit and loss account. The statement in Exhibit 32 has been prepared from the comparative balance sheet of Fairmaid Corporation (India) Ltd. (Exhibit 29) without reference to the company's profit and loss account for the year in question.

CHAPTER 26

Statement of Sources and Applications of Funds

The cash-flow statement, the statement of changes in net working capital, and the statement accounting for variations in owners' equity, or the net worth of a business, are all special purpose statements. For one thing, these are based on a restricted definition of the term "Funds" and, for another, they are designed to provide answers only to specific questions regarding the changes in the financial status of a business enterprise revealed by its balance sheet.

For common use and, more particularly, for reporting to owners, shareholders and creditors, a general purpose statement employing the broadest possible definition of the term "Funds" needs to be prepared for providing more complete and informative a picture of the financial affairs of a business.

Unlike the other statements, such an all-purpose statement does not exclude from its purview any of the information provided by the basic financial statements and presents a picture of the financial status of a business which is a comprehensive whole. Such a statement is designated the Funds Statement or the Statement of Sources and Applications of Funds.

It is to be appreciated that a balance sheet presented in the vertical form suggested by Schedule VI of the Companies Act is not a Funds Statement even though it employs in its format terms Sources of Funds and Applications of Funds (Exhibit 33). Admittedly, the balance sheet and the many annexures, schedules, and notes appended to it, do carry a wealth of information about several aspects of a company's financial status besides providing explanations of the accounting policies followed and other matters of importance. But, even careful reading of the document often fails to secure answers to the questions the reader may have in mind or to explain the situations he may find confusing.

Though much condensed in form and utilising the same information as is carried by the two basic financial statements, the Funds Statement is capable of explaining how the activities of a business have been financed and how the financial resources have been used during the period covered by the principal statements. It needs to be noted here that the Funds Statement is not yet another schedule appended to the balance sheet and the profit and loss account. It is a statement complementary to the principal statements and "an important document in its own right".

Exhibit 33

MULTI PRODUCTS LIMITED
Balance Sheet as at 31 March, 20__

	Schedule	Rs Lakhs	20__ Rs Lakhs	20__ Rs Lakhs
I. SOURCES OF FUNDS:				
SHAREHOLDERS' FUNDS:				
Capital	I			
Share Application Money pending allotment				
Reserves and Surplus	II		_____	_____
LOAN FUNDS	III		_____	_____
Total				
			=======	=======
II. APPLICATION OF FUNDS:				
FIXED ASSETS	IV			
CAPITAL WORK-IN-PROGRESS			_____	_____
INVESTMENTS	V			
NET CURRENT ASSETS:				
Current Assets, Loans and Advances	VI			
Less: Current Liabilities and Provisions	VII		_____	_____
MISCELLANEOUS EXPENDITURE (TO THE EXTENT NOT WRITTEN OFF OR ADJUSTED)	VIII		_____	_____
Total				
			=======	=======
NOTES ON ACCOUNTS	XIV			

(Figures have been omitted for the sake of convenience)

To prepare a funds statements all that the analyst need have is a comparative balance sheet showing the net changes which may have taken place in individual items during an accounting period. A comparative profit and loss account is useful but not indispensable though, for a more complete analysis, information regarding the net profit or loss earned and the amounts distributed as dividends is essential.

The analyst subjects the available information to elimination, combination, and reclassification, and presents it in a statement form made up of two parts (1) sources of funds, and (2) uses, applications, or dispositions of funds (Exhibit 34).

Exhibit 34

Source and Application of Funds Year ended 31 December 2001

(Rupees crore)

	2001	2000
Cash and marketable securities – beginning of the year	8.38	2.83
Source of Funds		
Profit after tax	6.18	11.36
Depreciation and depletion	6.44	6.88
New Borrowings	25.73	1.78
Increase/(Decrease) in bank borrowings	(0.31)	3.03
Others	0.65	(0.02)
	38.69	23.03
	47.07	25.86
Application of Funds		
Dividend	4.55	4.55
Capital Expenditure	11.86	8.27
Increase in working capital	16.01	3.45
Debt repayments	8.31	1.21
	40.73	17.48
Cash and Marketable securities – end of the year	6.34	8.38
	47.07	25.86

Sources of Funds

The funds deployed in any business concern come, or are received and secured from four basic sources: (1) profits earned from operations, (2) increases in liabilities, (3) decreases in assets, and (4) increase in share capital.

The net profit earned from operations is used partly to declare and pay a dividend and partly to strengthen the financial base of the business by addition to accumulated reserves. The latter is reflected in an increase in the owners' equity, more particularly as an accretion to revenue reserves. When this happens, a corresponding decrease has to take place in the liabilities or a partial change in the assets and in the liabilities.

An expansion in liabilities indicates increased use being made of borrowed funds or, as in the case of sundry creditors or accrued expenses, a temporary withholding of cash till liabilities mature and must be met. Short-term and long-term borrowings increase cash fund and are a source of working capital.

An increase in liabilities must be accompanied by either an increase in one or more of the assets or by a decrease in some other liabilities. For instance, a long-term loan may be raised to construct a new factory, or the bank overdraft or cash credit may be enlarged to pay suppliers bills or accrued expenses.

A decrease in assets will not necessarily go to increase the cash funds employed in the business since a decrease in some of the assets may be counter-balanced by an increase in some others. Whenever customers pay their dues, there is a decrease in the book value of outstanding debts, but there is an increase in the cash balance by a like amount. It is only when an asset, such as temporary investments, is sold at a profit that there will be an addition to the funds invested in the business to the extent of the profit realised.

For the purpose of construction of a statement of sources and applications of funds, a decrease in any asset or an increase in any liability is to be treated as a source of funds: any increase in an asset or a decrease in a liability to be considered an application of funds.

An increase in the share capital is not an every-day occurrence. But, when it does take place, it results in the introduction of additional cash funds or, occasionally, some asset or assets. On the balance sheet, the increase may appear as an increase in the capital and in the share premium account if the new shares are issued at a price in excess of their par value.

Non-cash Transactions

Besides cash transactions certain non-cash transactions also bring about decreases in assets or increases in liabilities or *vice-versa*. Such transactions include provisions for depreciation of fixed assets, depletion of wasting assets such as a mine or an oil well, amortisation of intangibles, and provisions or reserves for doubtful debts or advances, accrued income and expenses. Being non-cash in nature, they constitute neither a source nor an application of funds and, so, do not affect the cash balance in any way.

Yet, having been introduced into the picture by means of original adjustment and transfer journal entries, they do affect the final net profit, showing it lower than the true amount of cash resources generated by operations. To get a "true and fair picture", it becomes necessary to eliminate the effect on the net profit of non-cash transactions. This is done by "reversing" the adjustment and transfer journal entries which have introduced them in the first place.

There are two ways to attain the objective. The first, and more common, one is to add back to the reported net profit the amounts of the adjustments if they are in the nature of expenses, or to deduct their amounts if they are in the nature of income. The other way is to treat the adjustments as independent sources or applications of funds.

Uses of Funds

Funds obtained from the aforesaid sources may be applied or used to (1) offset the loss suffered during the accounting period, (2) increase assets, current as well as non-current, (3) decrease liabilities, current, non-current or deferred, and (4) to decrease tangible net worth or owners' equity by redeeming the preference share capital, if any.

If the net profit earned in an accounting period is a source of funds, it follows that a net loss assumed is an application of funds because when a loss is sustained, funds go out of the business to pay for expenses. If adequate reserves have been builtup during prosperous years, a resulting loss is written off against the accumulated reserves and, in that situation, the decrease in revenue reserves becomes an application of funds. But if adequate reserves are not available to absorb the loss, it must be offset by either a decrease in assets or an increase in liabilities (for instance short-term borrowings) either or both of which would be the source of funds provided for this particular application.

A decrease in liabilities, whether current or deferred, indicates an application of funds to pay creditors. The funds required for this application are provided by a decrease in assets or an increase in liabilities or net worth. A decrease in sundry creditors, for example, may be reflected in a decrease in cash, sundry debtors, or inventories, or an increase in bank overdraft. Long-term loans are often repaid by raising additional share capital which means an increase in tangible net worth.

When inventories, sundry debtors, investments, fixed assets or any of the other assets are increased, funds are used or applied. These funds may come from one or a combination of the four sources mentioned previously. When a new factory is built or the existing one is enlarged, cash is spent. But the cash itself might be provided by operations, long-term borrowings, or an issue of shares or debentures. Similarly, increases in incentives or sundry debtors may indicate investment of current profits or employment of funds provided by short-term lenders such as banks or trade creditors.

A decrease in tangible net worth takes place when operations during a period result in a loss or if the preference share capital is redeemed, in part or in full. Funds required for these applications are provided by operations or by cash balances built up in the past for the purpose of redemption of share capital. At times, the existing preference shares are redeemed by issuing another class of preference shares or equity shares9. In this situation no charge, of course, is brought about in the total of share capital.

The Funds Statements – Illustration

Pioneer Industries Limited

To construct a truly complete statement of funds, not only the comparative balance sheets as at two consecutive dates, or as at the start and at the end of a period, is necessary but also the profit and loss accounts for all of the intervening years to obtain the precise amounts of the profit (or loss) made, and the non-cash transactions and dividend payments effected. In the case of public limited companies whatever information is required is readily available from the published annual reports and the preparation of a comprehensive funds statement presents no difficulty.

In the case of private limited companies which are required to file their annual reports with the Registrars of Companies, however, the profit and loss account is not required to be included and it is not possible, therefore, to cast a fully informative funds statement. In this situation the funds statement usually takes the form of a statement of changes in Net Working Capital or a Statement Accounting for Changes in Owners' Equity or Net Worth.

The funds statement presented in Exhibit 38 has been prepared from the comparative balance sheet of Pioneer Industries Ltd. as at October 31, 2001 and 2002 (Exhibit 35) and the additional information, as mentioned in paragraphs 1-8 below, drawn from the profit and loss account for the year ended October 31, 2002, and the schedules and notes appended to the balance sheet and the profit and loss account.

A number of significant changes took place in the financial position of the company between October 31, 2001 and October 31, 2002. These were:

1. The Union Government and the High Court of Judicature at Bombay approved the merger of the erstwhile National Bank of India Ltd. with Pioneer Industries Ltd. As a result of the amalgamation, Pioneer Industries Ltd. received a sum of Rs 290 lakh, a major part of which was utilised to finance a good portion of the capital expenditure during the year.

2. In accordance with the approved terms of the scheme of amalgamation, 12,42,825 equity shares of Rs 10 each and 8% convertible bonds of Rs 6 each aggregating Rs 75.1 lakh were issued to the shareholders of the National Bank of India Ltd.

Exhibit 35

PIONEER INDUSTRIES LIMITED
Comparative Balance Sheet as at October 31, 2001 and 2002

Items	2001	2002	Change
	(Rupees in Lakhs)		
ASSETS			
Current Assets			
Cash	29.6	19.7	-9.9
Marketable Securities	5.0	5.0	-
Sundry Debtors – Gross	677.9	515.3	-162.6
Inventories	868.6	974.0	+105.4
Prepaid expenses	18.3	51.7	+33.4
Deposits	3.3	23.9	+20.6
Other Current Assets	111.1	8.26	-28.5
Total Current Assets	1713.8	1672.2	-41.6

Items	2001	2002	Change
	(Rupees in Lakhs)		
LIABILITIES & NET WORTH			
Current Liabilities			
Acceptances	177.1	159.5	-17.6
Sundry Creditors	767.2	746.2	-21.0
Short-term Loans	809.2	558.2	-251.0
Accrued Interest	20.1	18.7	-1.4
Provision for – Taxation	43.2	89.6	+46.4
– Bad Debts	5.3	7.1	+1.8
Other Current Liabilities	7.0	4.2	-2.8
Total Current Liabilities	1829.1	1583.5	-245.6

Contd....

Exhibit 35 (Contd...)

PIONEER INDUSTRIES LIMITED
Comparative Balance Sheet as at October 31, 2001 and 2002

Items	2001	2002	Change
			(Rupees in Lakhs)
Fixed Assets :			
Buildings, Plant & Equipment	615.9	1009.0	+393.1
Deduct – Depreciation	248.5	326.9	+78.4
Fixed Assets – Net	367.4	682.1	+314.7
Add – Land	46.2	46.2	-
Capital Work-in-progress	202.3	58.4	-143.9
Total Fixed Assets – Net	615.9	786.7	+170.8
Long-term Investments	242.1	247.3	+5.2
Advances to Subsidiaries and Affiliates	42.7	79.8	+37.1
Miscellaneous Assets	175.8	182.5	+6.7
TOTAL ASSETS	2790.3	2968.5	+178.2

Items	2001	2002	Change
			(Rupees in Lakhs)
Long-term Loans	304.1	380.3	+76.2
Total Liabilities	2133.2	1963.8	-169.4
Net Worth			
Share Capital – Preference	43.0	37.0	-6.0
– Equity	316.8	441.1	+124.3
Total Share Capital	359.8	478.1	+118.3
Reserves – Capital	19.0	115.7	+96.7
– Revenue	278.3	410.9	+132.6
Total Reserves	297.3	526.6	+229.3
Total Net Worth	657.1	1004.7	+347.6
TOTAL LIABILITIES & NET WORTH	2790.3	2968.5	+178.2

3. A further six thousand 8.45% redeemable cumulative preference shares of Rs 100 each were redeemed during the year and a sum of Rs 6,00,000 was transferred from the General Reserve to the Preference Shares Redemption Reserve.

4. The amalgamation resulted in the creation of a capital surplus of Rs 96.7 lakh of which Rs 62.1 lakh were placed to the credit of a Share Premium Reserve and the balance in an Amalgamation Reserve pending clarification of certain legal points.

5. The final net profit for the year ended October 31, 2002 was Rs 175 lakh inclusive of Rs 20 lakh provided for contingencies and Rs 19.5 lakh for retiring gratuities.

6. Dividends in respect of the year ended October 31, 2001 distributed during the year amounted to Rs 45.2 lakh inclusive of Rs 6,83,554 paid out of reserves.

7. Excess provisions and sundry accounts written back to reserves totalled Rs 8,82,214.

8. Depreciation written off fixed assets during the year was Rs 87.4 lakh and the difference of approximately Rs 9,00,000 probably represented adjustment on account of retirement of fixed assets.

Preparing the Funds Statement

Using the comparative balance sheet shown in Exhibit 35 and the additional information given above, a detailed funds statement for the year ended October 31, 2002 can be compiled in three successive steps.

As the first step in the compilation, a detailed preliminary funds statement is prepared as in Exhibit 36 (Parts A and B) by listing each of the items in the increase/decease column of the comparative balance sheet in Exhibit 35, as either a source or an application of funds. Under sources are shown decreases in assets, increases in liabilities and increases in net worth. Under applications are listed increases in assets, decreases in liabilities and decreases in net worth.

According to this statement, total funds obtained from different sources aggregated Rs 679 lakh, the largest contribution coming from the increase in the net worth. Of these funds, Rs 379.2 lakh were used, or applied, to increase assets, Rs 293.8 lakh to decrease liabilities, and Rs 6.0 lakh were used to redeem a part of the preference capital. Total applications aggregated Rs 679 lakh and balanced total of sources.

Exhibit 36-A

PIONEER INDUSTRIES LIMITED
**Detailed Preliminary Funds Statement for the Year ended
October 31, 2002**

Sources			Rupees in lakhs
Decreases in Assets:			
Cash		9.9	
Sundry Debtors		162.6	
Other Current Assets		28.5	201.0
Increases in Liabilities:			
Provision for : Taxation	46.4		
: Bad debts	1.8	48.2	
Long-term Loans		76.2	124.4
Increases in Net Worth:			
Equity Share Capital		124.3	
Capital Reserves		96.7	
Revenue Reserves		132.6	353.6
TOTAL SOURCES OF FUNDS			679.0

Exhibit 36-B

PIONEER INDUSTRIES LIMITED
**Detailed Preliminary Funds Statement for the Year ended
October 31, 2002**

Sources			Rupees in lakhs
APPLICATIONS			
Increases in Assets:			
Inventories	105.4		
Prepaids	33.4		
Deposits	20.6		
		159.4	
Fixed Assets - Net		170.8	
Long-term investments		5.2	
Advances to Subsidiaries and Affiliates		37.1	
Miscellaneous Assets		6.7	379.2
Decreases in Liabilities:			
Acceptances	17.6		
Sundry Creditors	21.0		
Short-term Loans	251.0		
Accrued Interest	1.4		
Other Current Liabilities	2.8		293.8
Decrease in Net Worth:			
Preference Shares Redeemed			6.0
TOTAL APPLICATIONS OP FUNDS			679.0

Exhibit 37, the second step, is an intermediate statement wherein the various items in Exhibit 36 are rearranged in accordance with the more typical grouping of items in a balance sheet. At the same time, the net profit figure of Rs 175 lakh and the net increase of Rs 78.4 lakh in accumulated depreciation are introduced as sources of funds while Rs 45.2 lakh paid out as dividends and 249.2 lakh expended on acquisition of fixed asset are both inserted as applications of funds. Following these changes, both sources and applications of funds aggregated Rs 802.6 lakh.

The third and final statement in the series is presented as Exhibit 38. Increases and decreases in individual current assets and current liabilities have been removed and in their place has been introduced, in the applications portion of the statement the single item of increase in net working capital of Rs 204 lakh supported by two complementary

Exhibit 37

PIONEER INDUSTRIES LIMITED

Intermediate Funds Statement for the Year ended October 31, 2002

	Rs Lakhs	Rs Lakhs
SOURCES		
Current Assets		201.0
Current Liabilities		48.2
Long-term Loans		76.2
Increase in Accumulated Depreciation		
Provided during 2001-2002	87.4	
Less: Prior years' adjustment	9.0	78.4
Net Worth		
Equity Shares Capital	124.3	
Capital Reserves	96.7	
Revenue Reserves	2.8	223.8
Net Profit for the year		175.0
TOTAL SOURCES OF FUNDS		802.6
APPLICATIONS OF FUNDS		
Current Assets		159.4
Fixed Assets – Gross		249.2
Investment in and Advances to		
Subsidiaries & Affiliates		42.3
Miscellaneous Assets		6.7
Current Liabilities		293.8
Net Worth		
Preference Shares Redeemed		6.0
Dividends Paid		45.2
TOTAL APPLICATIONS OF FUNDS		802.6

Exhibit 38

PIONEER INDUSTRIES LIMITED
Final Funds Statement for the Year Ended October 31, 2002

	Rs Lakhs	Rs Lakhs
SOURCES		
Net Profit		175.0
Accumulated Depreciation		78.4
Long-term Loans		
8% Convertible Notes	75.1	
Others	1.1	
	76.2	
Increase in Net Worth		
Equity Shares issued	124.3	
Capital Reserves	96.7	
Revenue Reserves	2.8	
	223.8	
Less: Preference Shares Redeemed	6.0	217.8
TOTAL SOURCES OF FUNDS		547.4
APPLICATIONS OF FUNDS		
Dividends Paid		45.2
Increase in Net Working Capital:		
Increase in Current Liabilities	245.6	
Less: Decrease in Current Assets	41.6	204.0
Additions to Fixed Assets		249.2
Investments & Advances to Subsidiaries & Affiliates		42.3
Miscellaneous Assets		6.7
TOTAL APPLICATIONS OF FUNDS		547.4

items— (1) decrease in current liabilities of Rs 245.6 lakh, and (2) decrease in current assets of Rs 41.6 lakh. Likewise, increases and decreases in individual items of net worth have been brought together to give a single figure, on the sources side of the statement, of Rs 217.8 lakh as increase in net worth. The remaining items in the intermediate statement also have been regrouped.

The funds statement in its final form lists four sources of funds, namely, (i) net profit of Rs 175 lakh, (2) increase in accumulated depreciation of Rs 78.4 lakh, (3) increase in long-term loans of Rs 76.2 lakh, and (4) increase in net worth of Rs 217.8 lakh. According to this statement, funds provided by the four sources totalled Rs 547.4 lakh.

On the applications side, there are five items— (1) dividends paid of Rs 45.2 lakh, (2) increase in net working capital of Rs 204 lakh, (3) additions to fixed assets worth Rs 249.2 lakh, (4) increase of 42.3. lakh in investments and advances to subsidiary companies and affiliates, and (5) increase in miscellaneous assets of Rs 6.7 lakh. Total applications also aggregated Rs 547.4 lakh as they should have.

Index